FOREVER CASH™

FOREVER CASH™

Break the Earn-Spend Cycle,
Take Charge of Your Life,
Build Everlasting WEALTH

JACK BOSCH

NEW YORK

FOREVER CASH™
Break the Earn-Spend Cycle, Take Charge
of Your Life, Build Everlasting WEALTH

ISBN 978-1-61448-782-1 paperback
ISBN 978-1-61448-783-8 eBook
Library of Congress Control Number: 2013912189

Morgan James Publishing
The Entrepreneurial Publisher
5 Penn Plaza, 23rd Floor,
New York City, New York 10001
(212) 655-5470 office • (516) 908-4496 fax
www.MorganJamesPublishing.com

Cover Design by:
Rachel Lopez
www.r2cdesign.com

Interior Design by:
Bonnie Bushman
bonnie@caboodlegraphics.com

In an effort to support local communities, raise awareness and funds, Morgan James Publishing donates a percentage of all book sales for the life of each book to Habitat for Humanity Peninsula and Greater Williamsburg.

Get involved today, visit
www.MorganJamesBuilds.com.

Habitat
for Humanity
Peninsula and
Greater Williamsburg
Building Partner

To my wife Michelle and daughter Sophia:
I couldn't be where I am
without you next to me!

And to my parents:
You had the courage to support me
even though I went the unbeaten path.

CONTENTS

ACKNOWLEDGMENTS

This book would not have been possible without the help of all the people around me. There is no such thing as a self-made success. It is *always* a team-made success. I want to thank my family and, foremost, my wife Michelle for being on this journey next to me, often ahead of me, sometimes behind me, holding me up with her strength, and *always* ready to go down the road less traveled with me. Without her, I would probably be in some suffocating hamster wheel job in Germany, overworked and underpaid. Michelle is not just my partner in life, she is a brilliant business person on her own who powerfully and efficiently runs many of the most important parts of our companies. I want to thank my daughter Sophia for being an ever-smiling light in my life and my inspiration to be the best role model I can ever be. I might have not written this book without her, but I want her to have something that she and her kids can still read many years or decades from now. I want to thank my parents who, even though they are an ocean away from me, have always believed in me and were willing to support me—love you guys! I also want to thank my brother who, when I was frustrated at my job and didn't see the light, told me to keep focused on finding a way.

And, of course, I want to thank my team at our investment and education companies. I owe a great deal of gratitude particularly to Alex Delacruz and Christine Mclaurin, but also to all those who have come and gone over the years in our business. Christine, thank you for always trusting Michelle and me for more than nine years now. You are a true rock on which we can rely. I don't know how you are able to do four jobs *as* one person, but you do it day in and day out. Alex, thank you for your creativity, dedication, and willingness to challenge me and my ideas to make them better. Thank you for finding solutions to situations and challenges I would have never been able to solve on my own. I fondly remember many evenings where we both sat on Skype in our respective home offices, figuring stuff out. Not only have you both been with me and Michelle for years as loyal companions in our real estate deals and educational ventures, you have materially contributed to this book with your ideas, reviews, and suggestions. Thanks also to our education support team and our advanced training team, which includes Henry Serrano, Tom Epperson, and Peter Sorensen. Thanks also to my team of amazing business advisors that is led by our CPA and friend Warren Taryle, who has saved us a small fortune in taxes, our attorney William Kozub, and many others who have materially helped over the years.

Thanks goes also to my editor Amanda Rooker and her team who have done a marvelous job taking my grammatically challenged English and converting it into something legible. Thanks also to everyone who has reviewed the book concept, the very rough manuscript, and given me their great feedback, including: Mike Decker; Tom and William Epperson; Darren Wilson; Kevin McCarthy; Gary Andrews; Adam Brooks; again, Alex Delacruz; and, of course, my wife Michelle. Your feedback, comments, and editing have sharpened the focus of the book, and I believe they have made the message clearer and more actionable.

And thanks to all who have contributed to my education, my success, and helped me become a better investor, better educator, and better business person; in particular, I want to thank Armand Morin,

Matt Bacack, Ron LeGrand, Francis Ablola, Ray Edwards, the AM2 Platinum community, and many more who don't even know I have learned from them.

Finally, to my publisher Morgan James Publishing: thanks for believing in this message and bringing it into the world. I am confident it will change many people's lives. To my clients, customers, followers, and Forever Cash adventurers, may this book be a light to a brighter future.

INTRODUCTION

Welcome to Forever Cash™. The fact that you purchased and opened this book, or that someone was thoughtful enough to give it to you means that you probably are not happy with where you are in your financial life. I want to make a commitment to you here, right now, at the beginning.

It is my goal to challenge the way you think about money, about how money is being made, and about what retirement means. It is my sincerest hope that when you have completed this book, you will examine your life from a different angle—that however slightly different that angle is, it will revolutionize how you work with money, earn money, and spend money.

Furthermore, I am daring you to throw aside your old thought patterns about the subjects of money, wealth, and retirement. I want you to open your mind to the possibility that there is an entirely different way to think about these subjects.

Yes, I will show you how to think about money, where it comes from, how it is created, and how it is meant to be used. Most likely, what you read here will stir you up a bit. And—if I do my job well—it will show you how much time and money you have already wasted going down the wrong path.

But don't worry. If you plan to live a few more years, you can absolutely right the ship and get on the fast lane to a retirement that might be just a few short years from now. It doesn't matter where you start from.

It is my commitment that, in this book, I am not giving you a repetition of the same tired advice and platitudes that the American middle class has been fed for decades. Obviously, if that advice worked, the middle class—and even the more affluent higher income class—wouldn't be struggling with debt and worrying about retirement.

This book is not filled with ways to "get rich quickly" or "quit your job and pour your life savings into a business you know nothing about." Instead, my techniques and process to get you from where you are now to financial security forever are easy to grasp, but they will take effort and time to make them work. At the end of this book, however, it will show you how to become financially secure and even how to stay rich *forever*.

Have you ever had any of these or related thoughts?

- Do you feel like you are in a big hamster wheel of financial hell? As you get older, you make more money; you buy more stuff; you get into more debt; and you become more dependent on a job—particularly if the job is high paying. Soon, you are married with two kids; you can't afford to let go of that job; and—although you might not like what you do day in and day out—you don't see a way out.
- You feel trapped, and you think this is normal because everyone else seems to be in the same situation.
- Do you feel like you are treading water financially, not getting ahead no matter what you do?

- Are you starting to realize that with life comes costs and you are drowning in expenses?
- Is the income from your 9–5 job not enough to let you afford the lifestyle you want and not enough to even think about getting ahead or planning for retirement?
- Are you making good money and have nothing to show for it other than a house, a collection of expensive toys, and a mountain of debt—and you feel trapped in the cycle of earn to spend?
- Do you have dreams of quitting your job and being financially independent and secure yet you have no clue where to even start to get there?
- If you are close to retirement, are you going to be able to live as well as you would like to, and will you be able to enjoy your current standard of living?

And finally: Are you sick and tired of being lied to by all the media, the banks, the financial advice industry, and even, for that matter, the school system, telling you that all will be well if you just get a good education, get a good job, invest in a good 401k and a good mutual fund, and work forty years of five days a week with two days off each week, and two weeks of vacation?

If you *are* sick and tired of this lie, then read on. You will find a strategy that has been around for centuries, but only among the wealthy of this world. And it has to my knowledge never been taught and shared in this way. It can and, if applied, will help you break out of this process of giving most of your life to an employer that doesn't care about you, and it will allow you to take charge of your life and your family and become the provider you are meant to be, whether you are a man or a woman.

And unlike other books that offer financial advice, I am not going to ask you to deprive yourself of all fun activities that cost money. I am not a fan of cutting up credit cards, and drastically reducing the quality of your life. If you like buying a Starbucks coffee each day and it makes you feel good, I say do it. If you like cable TV, I say keep your subscription. If you like eating out, continue doing so. I don't believe in you reducing your quality of life substantially over the long term. Of course, cutting your everyday expenses could advance you faster by freeing up more money, but cutting out every single thing that makes you enjoy life will sap the life and motivation out of most people. Life is just no fun without having at least some nice amenities—like a dinner out, cable TV (if that is important to you), and the occasional Starbucks coffee. I will, however, make a point to ask you to look at your expenses in detail, decide which ones serve a purpose, which ones don't serve a purpose, and to stop throwing money away on things that don't bring you forward at all.

And I am also not going to recommend to you that you drop everything and risk your life savings and start a business. Mark Cuban, owner of the Dallas Mavericks and well-known entrepreneur, said:

> In business, to be a success, you only have to be right once. One single solitary time, and you are set for life. That's the beauty of the business world.[1]

Many financial advice books would agree with him and therefore recommend you put all you have on the line and swing for the fences in the hopes of making it big. And while I, too, agree that this is a way to go, the reality that I have observed is that too many people spend their entire lives waiting for that "one win," only to lose it all and—in the process—sacrifice so much of what's important to them, like family and friends. I have friends who are on their tenth start-up company, waiting to "strike it rich," who have spent the last twenty years chasing that "one" big success. Often, they have even started their own start-up company just to see it end in nothing soon after (taking with it their life savings).

That is not my style, and it's not how I made my money. And I don't think it is the right path for most of the people reading this book. It is my experience that, just like I had no clue how to start my own business (and I had a business degree), most people don't have the know-how on how to start and run a successful business right now. So, while in this book I will show you a path to you quitting your job in possibly as little as one to three years from now, I will show you a path that does not necessarily include (unless you want it to) leaving everything behind to work for a start-up with minimal chances of success.

The rich think differently than the average people. Average people think that it takes money to make money, the rich know that you don't need money to make money, and instead that you need to have specific knowledge to get wealthy. Those who have or acquire that mindset and knowledge will be able to make money anytime, anywhere.

So I would challenge you to at least open your mind to the possibility that there is a path for you out of your current life situation and towards financial independence without having to risk everything.

Lots of people do it all the time, and you can too, by generating lots on smaller and larger "wins" that in turn can, within a few short years, absolutely lead to you being financially independent and secure. And if applied for just a bit longer after you become financially safe and secure, you can be living a life with an abundance of cash coming in *forever* (think two to five and even ten times what you are making now as a distinct possibility).

This book is written to help you become a Money Master in a methodical, easy to grasp and easy to do way. All it takes is to understand how the people who have *created, kept,* and *expanded* their wealth have done it. And what you will find is that they diligently follow a simple approach. Yet, almost nobody has ever talked about that approach in public.

And when you are a Money Master, life takes on a different quality. It has been true in my case and in the case of every person I have ever met who has diligently applied the principles and actions described in this book.

So, are you ready?

Chapter 1

WHY AM I WRITING
THIS BOOK NOW?

I am writing this book because I am tired of seeing people around me suffering, struggling, and not getting ahead. I am tired of seeing good, hard-working people being given bad advice and realizing they do not even *know* they are getting bad advice. I am tired of seeing people following the conventional wisdom, which means they are doing what everyone else is doing and not asking whether that "conventional wisdom" is the best way to go.

I understand all of this, and it motivated me to help.

For a time, I subscribed to that conventional wisdom, too, and I didn't even think or consider that there might be a different model out there. But there *is*. Once I saw that model, once I realized that it was possible to get to a different, better financial place in life, and *stay* there, it was almost as if my wife Michelle and I saw and entered a parallel universe. It wasn't always easy, and we made many mistakes. These mistakes cost us money along the way, but we learned from our mistakes and moved forward. Once we made the decision to stay focused on our goals, there was no going back.

There is a difference between those who make a great deal of money and those who have built lasting wealth. As a matter of fact, it doesn't even take much money to create lasting wealth, but it requires seeing the world from a different angle and in a different light.

Once you change your way of looking at and thinking about the steps to financial security, the steps that lead to independence and freedom from money worries will become the only logical steps for you to take. When you see the world in that way, you will see opportunity where everyone else sees problems. You will get excited when other people get frustrated. You see the light when others only see the darkness. It's actually quite amazing.

Once you understand the power of all this knowledge and enlightenment, you will also be able to see *through* the messages you are getting from the media, the banks, the financial advice industry, and the school system—all of whom knowingly or unknowingly (because they just don't know any better) operate together to keep you blind and following their *bad* advice. They control the message you hear through virtually all communication channels, and they make sure you never hear something that deviates from what they preach. Honestly, it is mostly bad advice that has been primarily designed to help *them*, and it is advice that will just keep *you* treading water.

I am also writing this book because I think it is time for you to stand up and take charge of what is yours. Take charge of your financial life and of your family. Just handing the money over to advisors (most are ill-suited to represent your best interest) is the cheap way, and a way that is not in *your* best interest.

It's time for you to go against the grain and do what needs to be done to get financially free *forever.*

I am also writing this book because even the people who have figured out how to make a ton of money are often missing the *one* crucial step to their true financial independence.

For several years now, I have been teaching other people the actual money-making techniques that made me wealthy. As I taught people these simple—yet lucrative—investment techniques, what I saw was that people used my techniques successfully to also generate a lot of cash, and then they used the cash to buy themselves the things they always wanted—the cars, the house, the vacations....

After they spent that income, however, the cash was gone, and they had to go back and work some more deals. While there is nothing wrong with improving your lifestyle dramatically while being able to quit your job, they still had nothing to show for it, other than a lot of money spent and having lived "large" for a while. Many people would argue that this is what life is all about. Just making more money is *not* the full picture. Nobody has told them that there is another step that leads to the ultimate freedom of never having to work again—unless you want to.

In fact, most people *never* realize that there is a second step after you make that money that truly ensures financial independence forever. That second step is to use the money they made and create an ever- growing amount of Forever Cash. This kind of cash will keep them and their families financially safe, secure, and independent—for not just their lifetime, but the lifetimes of their kids and grandkids, too.

It is time to break the "make money to spend money" cycle, the one you're no doubt in.

It breaks my heart, and it makes me *mad,* because every single person who understood how money really works could be retired, living in comfort or even in luxury for years, if they just understood how the rich *stay* rich, and how they *work* and *keep* their money. It's simply part of what financial education should be. The rich *work their money;* they do *not* work *for* their money. Actually, that is part of the structure of this path and of my philosophy to creating lasting wealth.

No one teaches these principles today, and it certainly is not being taught in school. Think about it. If we include preschool, kindergarten, and perhaps college for some of us, we spend a good fifteen to twenty years of our lives in school learning all kinds of things, from the sciences (like biology, chemistry, and physics) to languages and history. These subjects are all essential pieces of a well-rounded individual.

After graduation, however, we are sent out into the world, and we spend almost the rest of our lives trying to do this thing called "make money," a subject about which we have learned absolutely nothing in school. It's no wonder that so many people struggle in this area of life even if they are lucky enough to bring home big paychecks. For some people, even if they manage to make a large amount of money, they tend to lose it all within a short time. Why? The answer is simple: They don't know the rules of money and how to create ongoing streams of income that last forever.

This is the crux of what we are talking about:—the creation of ongoing streams of income. How far you take the things you learn depends on how diligently you apply them, how you internalize the way of thinking behind the philosophy and specific methods, what your goals are, and what vehicle you choose to accomplish your goals. I can promise you, however, that *if* you apply the lessons diligently, you can (within a few short years) reach a state of financial peace of mind for the rest of your life. You will know that you and your family will never have to worry about being able to pay your bills again, and if you continue to apply it after that, there is no way you won't be incredibly wealthy over time. It's how the world works; it's a financial law.

Chapter 2

MY PATH TO
FINANCIAL
INDEPENDENCE

I t was a beautiful Arizona day in late 2000. I was working for a company that—in 1999—had been listed as #1 on the "100 fastest-growing companies" list by *Forbes Magazine*. It was a software company, and I was working as an implementation consultant.

Just a few years earlier, I had come to the United States from Germany with nothing more than two suitcases, my college admissions papers, and big hopes.

Through a stroke of luck, I had, after completing college, scored a job at this software company and—on the surface—everything looked great. As part of my job, I traveled across the United States, lived in nice hotels, and ate at good restaurants—all on a comfortable expense account. On top of that, I had been given some stock options that were vesting over five years, and that had the potential to be worth up to $300,000 at the then-current stock price. If you had been an observer of my life at that time and looked at the way I was living and working, you would have thought that things were looking rosy for me and my future.

However, that was not the case at all. As a matter of fact, I was absolutely miserable.

On the positive front, I had just gotten engaged to Michelle (now, happily, my wife), and we were living in Phoenix, Arizona. But on the negative side, although I had an apartment in Phoenix, I was away traveling 100 percent of the time (from Sunday night to Friday night) and hating every single minute of it.

When I was in town on weekends, I was spending the time more or less sleeping—just recovering from the week—and did little else. At my job, we were working 60 to 80 hours a week (literally 12 to 15 hours a day, from 8 a.m. to sometimes midnight) often without stopping even for the weekend. And all that traveling that I was doing? In all of those different cities that I was visiting, I basically only saw the airport, the highways on the way to the hotel, the hotel bar (the only place that served food at the time we got out of the office), and a few lunch places that were close to whichever customer's office I was being sent to.

And instead of working in some of the world's most exciting, most dynamic metropolitan areas, I was sent to places like small towns in Wisconsin—during the *winter*. Now, even though Wisconsin's a great place, it's just not what I thought of as an exciting place to visit. When I did finally get sent to some of the big cities, I found that—almost always—the customers were located in boring suburbs where *nothing* of *any* interest was happening. Needless to say, it made me think about my life. I mean, this was hardly how I had envisioned the start of my career to be. When I arrived in the United States, I had a completely different vision of what my life would be like after college. And—absolutely—my job and my life looked good to my neighbors and friends, but the reality was that I was utterly miserable.

Here it was in a nutshell: I was away from the person I truly cared about; I was working longer hours than I had ever anticipated; and, to top it all off, I was having to demonstrate expertise in an area that I always felt I had to struggle my way through throughout the day, learning all that software stuff on the fly, always hoping to be able to stay just one step ahead of the clients in the quickly and ever-changing world of technology.

In 2000, I had only been in the United States for three years. I had come from Germany, and this job had allowed me to stay in the United States and work on getting my permanent residency. As I soon realized, however, the only way to make a career in that company was to become either an expert in all things even remotely related to software architecture or to become a practice manager (which meant sales), and I had no knowledge, or desire, to learn the nuances of the business to that degree, nor to bank any more hours than I was already putting in. I felt like my place in the company wasn't looking as great as it once had. Here I was, two years out of college with a business major, and I was stuck in a technology company, with no way to leave.

To top it all off, the world's economy had just taken a turn for the worse in the form of the bursting of the dot-com bubble. Stock prices were in free fall and my stock options had lost almost all their value before I could exercise them. All the technology sector companies were changing paths and starting to lay off massive numbers of employees. The job that I had put all my confidence in, that I had looked to for my security, was on the verge of disappearing. There began to be talk of layoffs.

I was in a tough spot. As much as I now disliked being in that corporate position, this job was also my ticket to get permanent residency (also known as a "green card"), meaning that it was my ticket to being able to stay in the United States for the rest of my life, something I wanted. This also meant I had to stay with that company for as long as it took to get that green card (which, in my case, was 5½ years). I couldn't switch jobs without possibly having to restart my green card application from scratch. I couldn't afford to lose my job, because losing it would have meant I would have had sixty days to find a new job, or I would have had to leave the country.

What I feared that fateful day in the year 2000 came true. In just one day, my company let go of 1,000 people, reducing the work force from roughly 7,000 people to just 6,000 people. And they repeated that two more times in the next two years, reducing the number of people working for that company to just more than 4,500. But, on that day, as I was in the office looking out the window, having truly and literally nothing to do (other than some continued education), and offering my help to anyone who would listen to me (to make me look good and avoid being fired), I remember talking to a colleague who was husband to a lovely wife and father to a few children, one a child with special needs.

Because I was traveling so much, the two of us had never had a chance to get to know each other as I would have liked. That morning, however, for the first time ever, we talked, and he told me about his family. He left to take his lunch break. During that time, he also needed to take his daughter to the doctor as part of her regular therapy. We agreed to get together in the office after lunch for a cup of coffee and to chat some more. Then he left. I expected he would be gone for a few hours, and then just get some work done later (a freedom we had). Ten minutes later, however, he was back. When I asked him what was going on, he told me that he had just been let go, over the phone, by his manager, who lived in another city.

His news hit me like a ton of bricks. I was shocked.

At that moment, I realized no one was safe. No one. I realized there was no such thing as job security anymore—no matter how good that job looks on paper.

I realized that I (whether I wanted to or not) must take my life in my own hands and make something out of it. I needed something where I did not have to rely on a company that could fire me any moment.

I will always remember that day, because on that day something in me shifted. I wanted to get out of a job. I wanted to take charge of my own life. I wanted to have abundance in my life without having to work for "the man," and I didn't want to live in the ever-present dread and fear of being fired.

Before that day, literally all I wanted to do with my work life was to be an employee and make a career in Corporate America. I had accepted the conventional wisdom that we all have to work forty years to "earn" our retirement and then to retire in peace, living off our nest egg. I thought that the only way to retire was to be a good employee somewhere and to trust that the system wouldn't fail me if I just did my part. But after that day, I knew that was not the way to go. I had seen the face of Corporate America, and I knew I did not want to depend on the mercy of some higher-up corporate person to decide whether I will stay or go, and when.

Let me add here that—in spite of my personal feelings that I was never a good enough expert—I do think I provided a decent output at my job, and I do think that my hard work might have been the reason why I wasn't fired. But then again, most of my colleagues also produced well. I know that all of that may not have mattered for the silliest reasons. For example, if I would have not gotten along with my boss, my name easily could have gone from the "keep" list to top of the "fire" list. Sometimes, something as minor as a small personal difference or one bad customer review can make the distinction between keeping a job and looking for a new one.

I am sure you know exactly what I am talking about. Life is sometimes unfair—and this was one of those moments. Yet my employer didn't have a choice. This is just how capitalism works. In a downturn it's either keep the employees and go bankrupt, or let some (or maybe quite a few) go and survive as a company until the economy picks up or until the business model gets adjusted. I am a capitalist, and I understand how this works.

But I learned something that day.

While the *company* often does not have a choice when letting people go, I realized that *we* have a choice.

We have a choice between either submitting ourselves to the mercy of an employer who can fire us at any time, or we can start to build something outside our jobs that will make us financially secure forever.

For me, it was time to stand up and to start taking charge of my own family without depending forever on a *job*.

I think it is now time for more workers to stop being passively dependent on that company paycheck. More people should take the steps to do what it takes to make sure their families are financially safe and secure from the hardships of life.

That was the conclusion I came to at that moment. After that day, I took some time to review the things I had been told. I started to do some real soul searching. What I found was the following.

It's okay to march to the beat of your own drummer and to break out of the system that is designed to keep you passive and poor. As a matter of fact, this is the only way for most people to ultimately get what they want from life.

This book is not about getting rich. It is about *you* taking *your* life into *your* own hands and doing what needs to be done to make sure you and your family are safe. It's time to rise!

Since that day in the year 2000, I have been passionately consumed by the belief that there *is* a way to get things done and live a satisfying life, a life where you *can* have it all, no matter what other people say. If you decide you want to make your way in the world without depending on a large corporation, you can definitely do it.

Then I decided to take my future into my own hands. I wanted to live a life where I could offer my family the best, be there for my friends, and do what it takes to make that happen. For that, I was willing to change the way I was doing things. Are you at that point?

Yet, I had a problem. The problem was I could not just quit my job and jump into some business, because doing so would have canceled my application for permanent residency in the United States and would have effectively forced me to leave the country. I was stuck, or so I thought.

On top of all that, I had just started to do what people in this world do. I had bought a house, I had married my wonderful wife—and I started sinking deeper and deeper into debt. I had a mortgage, two car payments, and a great deal of consumer debt. Even if I did want to quit my job, I realized I wasn't in a position to do so at that time. I had to be realistic. What would I have to live on?

Yet, as I reflect on it now, I think the fact that I felt trapped—that I could not leave my job even if I wanted to do that right there and then—was a blessing in disguise. Because against my will (I wanted so much to just *quit!*), I was forced to find a way to make my dreams happen without immediately quitting my job.

I did just that. It took me some research and some trial and error, but once I found something I could do part-time outside my job and without having to be bound to a location, it took me only ten months to be able to quit my full-time job. It took me another eight months to be completely financially free and have assets of more than $1 million.

Not only that, but over several years my wife and I created a process that—if applied diligently—allows you to not just make a great deal of money but to also have more cash *forever* coming into your bank account, more funds than you could ever reasonably imagine having to spend on an ongoing basis. That "Forever Cash" is what ultimately set my wife and me free. That Forever Cash now allows us to travel the world and to spend three to four months a year on vacations and visiting family all over the world. When we come back to our Arizona home, we have more money in our bank account than we did when we left.

The fact that I could *not* quit my job back then helped me find a new way to freedom. It made me think. It made me conduct research. It challenged me to find a way to survive—and even *thrive*—without working for a big corporation and in a way that would not require me to quit my job right away. This new path to freedom for you is described in this book. It is a way that I have taught to many, with outstanding results. While many people would love to walk in and quit their jobs today, I had to learn to *use* my job as a short-term launching pad that finances and even speeds your path to financial security and independence.

I thoroughly refuse to accept the thought that to be successful you must work in a job for forty years, five days a week, with two weeks of vacation (the 5/2/2 rule), and put 10 percent of your money away into mutual funds or a 401k. Take a minute (if you need that long) and look around to see how well that is working for people. It is *not* working for most Americans—probably including you, if you are honest. Otherwise, you would have probably not picked up this book. And it didn't work for me either. Yet, I knew that there had to be a better way.

And while many people want to quit their jobs, quitting your job is scary if you have nothing to fall back on, no cushion. What I have proven is that you *can* do this part time—that is, if you just know what to look out for and how to *think* the way the truly wealthy do.

Being able to quit your job is ultimately one of the major goals for most, and we want to get there as quickly as possible. But it is not the *first* and most urgent goal for most. Neither is dropping everything and starting a new business. You see, many people and authors tell you to quit your job and start your own business. While it is proven that the fastest path to a great deal of wealth is starting a successful business, I don't agree with the notion these people spread that you *must* have a business to get free financially.

Look at my case as an example. I had a full-time job when I became financially free. It wasn't my job, however, that made me financially free. It was because I had figured out what to do *outside* of my job that made me financially free in a matter of ten months, just ten months after I determined a few basic principles of wealth creation and those of Forever Cash.

In my case, what I did was quite the opposite. I doubled up. I worked even harder than I ever had before—just to make sure I would *not* get fired, because I needed the money from the job to keep me afloat while my green card process continued, and while I was researching opportunities to make extra money. While still working at my job, I spent my evenings and some weekends doing online research and educating myself on all the opportunities to make extra money. I believed that the first part of any action is education. You will never know what you can do in life until you first look and learn and see what is possible. If inventors hadn't first seen birds fly, they would have never believed that mankind could one day fly, too. For many people, flying in an airplane is like driving in a bus. It's normal and millions do it every day.

Although I had a good education and a good job, I knew I had no idea how to make money outside of that job. I mean, just think about it. We are trained from a young age to grow up, to get a good education, and to get a good job. And that is what I did.

Having realized, however, that jobs were never designed to get you to a worry-free retirement—let alone an *early* retirement—I was struggling to find a way to make money on the side so I could quit my job as quickly as I could identify a source of profit.

The first step I took was to look for places where I could get training on where to start making more money. I took courses in real estate, online marketing, and also joined a network marketing company. While I did not make much money right away, I got some first-rate training through these programs, which I needed because I had no idea on what I wanted to do—at all.

During that process, I also researched opening a bakery, but I tossed that idea out quickly after realizing that I had to be in town all the time and that I had to start baking at 2 a.m. (and I am *not* a morning person). I looked at real estate investing, stock market investing, and any conceivable method of making money. After each one, I evaluated each opportunity based on the following four criteria:

- Can the opportunity make a great deal of money? (By design, certain niches, and ways to make money can only make a small amount of money and are not easily able to scale up from that.)
- Can it create passive income? (Passive income is where money comes in over longer periods of time without me actively having to do anything.)
- Can I do this remotely? (Remember that I had to travel for my job from Sunday to Friday each week, and I never knew where I would be three weeks into the future).
- Can it be done part-time? (For residency reasons, I could not yet quit my job).

Looking back, I am happy I could not quit my job immediately. I simply wasn't ready to do it. I wasn't ready in my financial education, I wasn't ready in my ability to see opportunities, and I wasn't ready in just about any other way you can think of. If I would have quit and cashed in the little bit that was in my 401k (and my now almost-worthless stock options) I would have most surely burned through that money looking for a business idea, and—at the end of it all— I probably would have ended up broke and looking for another job. But, because I did have a job, I was able to use that as my launching pad toward being able to climb out of the hamster wheel in a matter of a short time.

I already hear the critics saying: "Jack, you are really giving people false hope. People will go out and risk their life savings and then lose it all through some crazy business venture."

But, as you will see, that is not what I did and that is not what I suggest at all. As a matter of fact, what I suggest is the exact opposite. When my former employer let go 1,000 workers in that single day, I also internally quit. I decided that I would rather spend my time bringing *my* life forward than giving it all to a corporation that might decide to cut its ties with me at any time. That day, a process was also set in motion that has allowed my family and me to be safe financially, to be secure.

On October 17, 2003, less than three years after that fateful day and just ten short months after I finally had determined what method I was going to use to get financially free, I was able to quit my job at the tender age of 33 (my wife was 28). While still having a job, I had become financially independent. And now I have built up a Forever Cash Flow, with tens of thousands of dollars coming into my accounts.

When I worked at that company as an employee I had:

- Substantial (five-digit) student loans
- Thousands of dollars in credit card debt
- Two car payments
- One house payment
- Consumer loans that added up to almost $10,000 (and included items like my couch, my bed, my refrigerator, my water softener…)

The day I quit my job, I had paid off:

- All my consumer debt (credit cards, all the consumer loans)
- All my student debt
- One car payment

That means my overall expenses had dropped from $5,000 a month to around $3,000 a month.

On top of being free from consumer debt, I had built up:

- $5,000 a month coming in through a permanent monthly cash flow for years to come
- More than $50,000 cash in the bank (which—at that time—equaled about one year of living expenses)

In short, we reached this goal by playing financial *offense* (making more money) and *defense* (reducing our expenses while keeping our lifestyle the same).

Ten months later, we had:

- Paid off the mortgage on my house
- More than $12,000 a month in *permanent* passive cash payments coming in
- More than $1 million in assets!

As you can see, in less than two years after my wife and I had identified our path and started on it, we were totally debt free and financially secure.

It doesn't take that long to get out of what I call the "hamster wheel of financial hell." All it takes is some time to educate yourself and find what works for you. And then it takes a little action.

The day I quit my job was an exciting day *and* a scary day. After years in a job, it's easy to get used to that *false* sense of security that comes when you see a steady paycheck. The day had come, however, when it became too expensive to keep that job. We had reached a point where my wife and I, if we had stayed in corporate America (or in school for that matter), would be held back from generating more cash, more ongoing passive cash payments, and more profits, and from having more free time to spend with our loved ones.

In accomplishing all this, I also discovered that making money is only *one part* of the equation; the other part is keeping the money and turning the profits you made into even more profits—in other words, turning the cash you make into Forever Cash payments that come in for years and years, and ideally forever, regardless of whether you "work" at a 9-to-5 job.

It was the second part of this equation that brought my wife and I—and now our beautiful daughter, Sophia—the financial freedom and independence that we had been seeking. No matter how much money you do make, it won't be of any good if you don't know what money is supposed to be used for.

All it took was a slight shift in our thinking. We had to develop a different way of looking at money and how money (in my opinion) should be used. Yet, while this way of thinking about money has been around for as long as there has been money, most people don't know about it. Nor do the media and the financial institutions want you to know about them.

Chapter 3

WHAT IS YOUR NUMBER?

At the conferences I now speak at—some of which I am invited to, others of which I personally organize—people come up to me with the same story, and it goes like this:

"Hi, Jack. You know, about ten years ago, I was worth $1.4 million. And now, I'm having trouble just keeping up with the mortgage. I lost it all in a stock market crash [or by spending it unwisely, or by handing it over to someone who didn't have my best interest at heart]. I can't even bear to think about when I'll be able to retire. What can I do?"

Or I meet people who make $100,000, $200,000, or maybe even $500,000 in income per year, yet their credit cards are being declined when they want to buy dinner because they have more debt than income.

What happened?

They have just discovered that making a great deal of money doesn't equate to being able to live forever on a grand scale.

If they made their money quickly, they never learned to handle a great deal of money, and it went out as fast as it came in. For example, in 2009, *Sports Illustrated* estimated that 78 percent of NFL players are bankrupt or face serious financial stress within two years of ending their playing careers and that 60 percent of NBA players are broke within five years of retiring from the game.[2]

That is shocking, isn't it?

And for most people who made money slowly, through a high-paying "regular" job, (still following the conventional advice on what to do with it), that didn't work out for them, either. Most likely, these people were told that a full-time job equals security, and that the way to retire is to find a job with a large company and to put money into a 401k, or set up an IRA with one of the big brokerage firms and try to reach a magic number that will guarantee a comfortable retirement.

Or, if they had their own business, they were told they just needed to sell that business for a few million dollars and then all would be well forever. But then the business faltered and they lost all their money. The same would be true if they "made" their money through a lottery win.

What happened is that the conventional wisdom failed them, and now they feel lost because nearly everyone out there repeats the same advice that didn't work in the first place. Time and again, I meet people who can't find their way out, because they were never taught the right way to look at and use money.

The theory of building a pile of cash (also often known as "the number") that will last for life has not worked for most people. Unless you are extremely disciplined or that mountain of money is huge, it never has and it never *will* work. Just ask all those people who lost their money with Enron or in a huge market crash when they were ready to hit retirement. They can tell you.

The mountain of money or number theory claims that to be able to retire in style you need to reach a certain number, a certain dollar figure, or a certain size pile of cash in the bank that will last long enough. (And you don't want to outlive that!) While that is certainly one way to look at it, it has some serious flaws. One of these flaws is that the pile can disappear quickly if it is put in the wrong place and/or at the wrong time or with the wrong person.

Unless you are a star who makes millions a year, you probably have tried the conventional way of putting 10 percent of your paycheck away into a mutual fund or 401k. By now, you have probably realized that saving up a large pile of money will take forever.

But in the case of the people who speak to me at my seminars, making the money wasn't even the problem. They had all figured out how to make a great deal of money and to make it fairly quickly.

They knew how to *make* the money, but they did not know how to turn that money into *lasting wealth*.

So how to *use* the money you make is the most important part of this equation. It doesn't matter how *much* money you make, although making more speeds up the process. But what counts is what you *do* with it.

Investing is definitely the answer. But not just *any* investing! Investing in your 401k or IRA will almost certainly not bring you to your desired results. Have you ever noticed that the truly wealthy didn't make their money in mutual funds and usually only keep a small percentage in mutual funds? The plan to put 10 percent away and grow it is *not* what will give you the ability to retire early and with peace of mind. It's not designed to do that.

Knowing and understanding all this leads you to this question: What *kind* of investing is the solution?

What I am talking about is investing in assets that will make you— truly—financially free.

As I discovered this process and applied its principles to my life, I realized that this type of education was not being taught by schools, universities, and not even by most "get rich" programs. I had read one financial self-help book after another, and they simply didn't cover these lessons about money. As a matter of fact, most just teach the conventional wisdom stuff that hasn't worked for decades.

Are you ready to learn the secret of the wealthy? It might surprise you in its simplicity.

The secret of the wealthy is *Forever Cash* and *Forever Cash Flow!*

Truly wealthy people don't live off what their work pays; they don't rely on a job or even their businesses. Truly wealthy people live from the ongoing (forever) cash flow that their investments provide for them. They focus on creating such investments and then keeping them, preferably forever.

People who are already generationally wealthy don't work for money. They work just because they are passionate about something. They might work in a for-profit business, but their drive is not to make more money, but perhaps more influence or maybe it's something as basic as personal satisfaction. Some might work in nonprofits. Others might work to help the world be a better place. One thing is for certain, though: they don't work to make the money they need to live on. That part is taken care of *forever* and at a high level.

Look at Warren Buffett. He doesn't work for money anymore. He is actively giving his money away. For him, his work is his passion. As he famously said in 2008 when talking to business students from Emory and the University of Texas at Austin:

"I enjoy what I do. I tap dance to work every day."[3]

Where does the money come from for these generationally wealthy people? It comes from cash that gets deposited in their bank accounts each month year-in, year-out— without them having to work for it. Some of it might be invested in businesses (like Buffett does), but the point is that the wealthy people don't *have* to operate these businesses to make that money. The money comes in, no matter what they do day in and day out.

Even Warren Buffett doesn't operate any of the many businesses that his company Berkshire Hathaway owns. His "job" is to take the money these businesses throw off and reinvest it in the best possible way. While that sounds far-fetched for most people if they are drowning in bills and don't know where their money is going at the end of the month, it is possible for *anyone* to get to a place in life where all your ordinary—and even your extraordinary—expenses are covered by ongoing cash flow. All you have to do is to see how simple it is.

To accomplish the creation of this state of financial bliss, to make it happen for your life, you must be aware of how money works. If you don't learn how money works, you will be stuck, forever exchanging hours for dollars in the hopes that—through some lucky strike—you will suddenly wake up wealthy and be able to retire from your job. Let me give you a hint. It is not going to happen unless you take action and make some distinctions in your life. Begin by changing how you think about money and cash.

Chapter 4

NOT ALL CASH
IS CREATED EQUAL

Most people think of cash as, well, cash. It doesn't matter to them where it comes from. They see cash as something that is there to spend. To them, each dollar is the same. After all, a dollar is a dollar is a dollar. All $100 bills are green; they are the same size; they buy things.

But that is not *entirely* true. While the actual cash bill is the same, no matter where it comes from, it makes a huge difference *where* the money comes from, *how* it was generated, and how *often* it comes in.

To the rich, there are three different kinds of cash. In particular, they look at how cash is generated. In fact, your chance of retiring will depend on how well you understand what kinds of cash exist and what kinds of cash you pursue.

There are three different kinds of cash:

- One-Time Cash
- Temporary Cash
- Forever Cash

Which of the below three options do you think is best?
- $500 cash you received today for 10 hours of hard work you did last week
- $500 cash you received today in interest from a six-month, $50,000 private loan you gave to a real estate investor with 12 percent interest. It took you five hours to analyze the deal and complete the transaction, and now each month you just collect the $500 interest check. After six months, you get your $50,000 back and then find a new place to invest your money.
- $500 cash you received today from a rental house you bought last year. It took you five hours of work to complete the deal and rent the house, and now you receive $500 per month each month forever, doing nothing other than making a phone call to the property manager every few weeks to make sure things are going smoothly.

In each case, you receive $500 today. But are these three ways the same? Obviously not.

The reasons are clear:

First, the effort and kind of work to get the $500 in each case was quite different; and, second, the frequency of getting that $500 also is different and impacts the decision. In the first case, you received what I call "One-Time Cash." In the second case and third case, virtually no ongoing effort is required. In scenario two, you get $500 each month only for six months (and that's what I think of as "Temporary Cash"), but then you have to start again and find the next place to put your money. In the third case, you earn $500 cash that is *recurring* cash (what I like to call "Forever Cash") every month forever, and you no longer have to do *any* activity to earn that money other than managing the property manager with a couple of phone calls a month. You own an asset that spits out cash every month forever.

The rich have always understood this and receive all three types of cash. They occasionally will do something for a one-time fee, but they focus heavily on the second one and—particularly—on the last one. The poor class, the middle class, and even many of the more affluent job people and unenlightened entrepreneurs only receive one of them, that One-Time Cash. Let's look at each a little more closely. Each category is important for you to understand so that you can get to the place where you can actually break free financially!

One-Time Cash

One-Time Cash is what most people earn in their daily jobs. They work one hour and get one hour's pay. They work forty hours a week and get paid for forty hours a week. If someone asks you how much you are making at your job, and you answer $18 per hour, you are working (and living) in the One-Time Cash world.

One-Time Cash is the slow lane of wealth creation. Unless you are a highly specialized, highly sought-after expert—like a neurosurgeon or an attorney who specializes in a difficult area of the law—who can demand rates of hundreds, even thousands of dollars per hour, you are stuck. Even for these high-income earners (and certainly for you, too), your income has a clear limit. The most you technically can charge is twenty-four hours a day.

Once you give the value for that work (the hour, the project, the contract), you get paid for it, and you are out. There is no residual. You work forty hours a week, and you get a week's pay. You don't show up the next week; you don't get paid.

That is what One-Time Cash is all about. There is one product or service delivered, and one payment is made. That's it! However, even within One-Time Cash, there are differences in the quality of that One-Time Cash.

There are better ways of making One-Time Cash. For example, if you flip a house or a piece of land, you might make a $10,000 cash profit, and you might have worked only ten hours to make that happen. In this case, you still only get cash one time, but you get a much larger amount of cash than if you had worked in a job. Yet, to keep getting paid, you still have to keep doing deals and keep flipping more and more houses and/or land. Once *you* stop, the *money* stops.

That discovery was one of my first discoveries. When I started making money outside of my job, I selected tax delinquent real estate (where owners had not paid their property taxes) and land to focus on. My first twenty deals were all cash deals. I bought a property cheaply, for a few hundred or a few thousand dollars, and sold it for five to ten times as much in a few days. The first deal I ever made was a piece of land in a residential subdivision in northern Arizona. I bought it for $400 cash (with no mortgage) and sold it for $4,000 just one week after I bought it. The second one I bought for $500 and sold for $9,500 online in a matter of ten days, and so on. That continues to be something I do every day, but I soon realized I would have to keep flipping land forever if I wanted to keep the cash coming in.

That's when I discovered the power of Temporary Cash and Forever Cash.

Temporary Cash

Temporary Cash is an improvement from the One-Time Cash world, in that you work *once* and get paid again and again but only for a *limited, temporary* time.

For example, when you sell a piece of real estate with seller financing, you might get a 20 percent down payment from the buyer, and then you receive monthly payments for ten years. In some of the transactions, you can buy a piece of land in the outskirts of a major U.S. city for— let's say—$3,000 and sell it in a few days or a few weeks for $20,000. If you get a 20 percent down payment, you receive $4,000 down and then monthly payments of perhaps $300 for ten years.

Not only did you now get more as a down payment than you paid for the property (as a One-Time Cash down payment), but also for ten years, you get $300 in your mailbox every single month. Just think about that for a minute. You do fifteen such deals and you have $4,500 coming into your mailbox for ten years. Do thirty deals and you make over $100,000 a year in extra income!

There is still a problem, however. After ten years, the money stops.

If you want to retire forever, Temporary Cash is better than One-Time Cash. Once enough of it comes into your bank account, you can put up your feet for a few years. If you don't continue working, however, some day you will have to pick things back up and start creating more deals, creating more Temporary Cash.

I know you are familiar with this concept because you are a part of it every month in many ways. Unfortunately, you are on the wrong side of the game. Examples of this principle at work are your home mortgage, your car payment, and any online subscriptions you might have. Each and every month, you are being charged as part of a contract you have with another party/company. As a result, you are providing them with a stable, ongoing income that is not forever (you could always switch companies or refinance, you know) but it is usually for at least a few years at a time. Again, the problem is just that you are at the wrong end of the equation.

To be on the right end of the deal, you must set up income streams where people pay you. You could create Temporary Cash coming up with a service that people pay you monthly for but you only work once for. For example, if you wrote a book or a special report and published it through a portal like Amazon.com, you receive payments for the book sales every month for as long as the book sells. Now unless you write a book that becomes a classic, most books usually don't sell forever, so that wouldn't be considered Forever Cash, but you can reasonably expect that if the book meets any kind of a demand, you can sell it for two to three years and get checks every month for the sales generated. Yet, you only worked and wrote the book once.

You can also create Temporary Cash by selling something with installment payments. I just sold a motorcycle I had acquired by trading for services. When I sold it, I got $1,000 down and $200 a month for two years. That motorcycle costs me nothing more than some of my time to get, but now I receive cash flow from it for two years.

You can also start an online membership site for people who are interested in a particular subject. You provide great monthly value in the form of a newsletter, making it specific content they can use for their purposes, and they will pay you a fee for it. Many people have made a good living setting up two to three of these types of newsletters and having just fifty to a hundred paying interested parties, each paying anything from $29 to $99 a month. Anything can be made into a monthly membership site. There is even someone who offers prewritten sermons for priests and pastors in a membership-site format. When you think about it, it makes perfect sense. Pastors are busy people. With this service, they don't have to tear their hair out every week on a sermon. They can get ideas and even full sermons—ready to be used—from the membership site, which just charges a small monthly fee. Do you see how that works? It fills a need for them, and it provides income for the person who is hosting the membership site. If you just had 100 people sending you $30 a month, you would have $3,000 a month in extra income. And who knows or even cares if the same sermon is being used at the same time in some other church across the country?

Forever Cash

This is the true Holy Grail that will make you financially free forever. By now, you know that Forever Cash is cash for which you work *once* and get paid again and again and again … *forever.*

Forever Cash is what virtually all the people who are wealthy and who sustain their wealth use.

When in 2012, Bob Parsons, founder of GoDaddy.com, the Phoenix, Arizona-based webhosting company, sold a part of his company for $2.25 billion, the news got around. Phoenix radio show hosts started speculating with their listeners what Parsons might do with his money. And while only about $1 billion of the $2.25 billion was money Bob Parsons actually received and then had to pay taxes on, it is still more money than most people will ever see in their lifetime.

What I found interesting is that about six months after that transaction was complete, newspaper articles showed up reporting that Bob Parsons bought one apartment building and commercial property after another. So instead of *spending* his money, he *invested* a larger part of it into Forever Cash–producing assets so that no matter what happens to the rest of the money he will have cash flow coming in forever and can maintain whatever lifestyle he chooses. Not that it will, but now, even GoDaddy.com could go bankrupt, and Parsons will have cash flow coming in forever. Even if he loses the rest of his cash that is not invested, he will still have large cash flow streams coming to him from his Forever Cash Assets.

By funneling a portion of his assets and income into Forever Cash Assets, Parsons made certain he is set for life at a high level. That is the *power* of Forever Cash Assets. They provide cash flow for you, no matter what you do in life.

We can choose from a variety of other methods and Forever Cash Flow vehicles. The stock market provides several ways to create cash flow through dividend stock, or—if that doesn't produce enough— then by using more advanced option structures. There is cash flow through businesses like network marketing, particularly if the network marketing model includes some level of subscription or percentage payment on purchases you need anyway (like electricity, or day-to-day goods like gas, groceries, clothing, and even beer—the German in me is speaking). And there is, of course, real estate, which I still love—in spite of the 2008 crash. I love it because I never focused on what the masses did. I never participated in the house gold rush and never went and bought houses at market value in the hopes to sell them a few weeks later for more money. To me, that was never a sound investment; that was gambling. Instead, I have always been a purely cash flow investor. Yes, I have flipped quite a few properties, but only if I could buy them way below market value to make sure I have a margin of error and sell close to market value. And I only did that to generate the cash needed to then invest that into cash flow properties that spit out cash day in and day out. And what better times to invest in cash flow real estate than after a crash when the prices are low, yet rents are high. Many people have been shut out of the lending market due to financials or due to having had their house foreclosed on. Now, they need to rent to have a place to live. It's like a new gold rush, only the masses don't see it!

Examples of Forever Cash Flow–producing assets are:

- You own shares of an established, dividend-paying company that has been around for a long time and is profitable.
- You get paid forever for having created a network of subscribers for something people will need forever, like cell phones or electricity.
- You own farm land and lease it to a farmer.
- You own a rental house, an apartment complex, or a commercial property, and you lease it.
- You own and lease a piece of land to a cell phone company or a billboard company for their rights to put up a cell phone tower or a billboard.
- You own a piece of land with a mobile home on it. The owners of the mobile home pay you a land lease to have their mobile home on the property.
- You own a piece of an established limited partnership and get profit distributions each year. For as long as the partnership operates successfully (which could be forever), you get cash distributions every year.
- You have intellectual property and license it out for a monthly fee or, if it is product-related, for an ongoing royalty.

When you have built more Forever Cash than what you currently need to live on, you are truly financially secure and independent for your lifetime and even for past your lifetime. Think about Elvis Presley. Each year when they publish the "highest-earning artists of the year" Elvis is somewhere in there. And the guy has been dead since 1977! Talk about Forever Cash!

Just imagine for a moment that what I am saying here could be possible for you.

What if you could retire in a few short years from now with the same or more cash coming into your bank account than you have now from your job? How different would your life be? How differently would your kids and grandkids grow up then?

What if you start focusing not on who is winning on *American Idol* or *Survivor* but—instead—on how to create Forever Cash and what it would take to learn how to manage the Forever Cash in one to two hours a *week*?

If you were retired forever, would it be a big deal to manage thousands and tens of thousands of dollars coming into your bank account forever in one to two hours a week? Would it be worth spending a small part of your week learning how to do that?

All it takes is to learn a few rules and procedures. It's not difficult at all. But it does take the willingness to learn. If you could accomplish that, what example and principles would you instill on your kids and grandkids? Would you be the example of a parent who has to run to work each morning so you can make enough money to pay the bills? Or would you be a living example that life on your terms is possible? Would you be willing to accept that living the Forever Cash lifestyle and representing the Forever Cash philosophy is worth it?

Would you show your kids how you have to spend your hard-earned paycheck on a new car, or would you show them how to instead invest it in a "Forever Cash Asset" that, just like the Golden Goose from the fairy tale, lays golden eggs each day, week, month, and year forever, which then pays for the car?

You can follow this new way of thinking and this way of living your life and retire a few years from now in style, or you can do nothing and continue your path of earning and spending it all (or putting 10 percent in your 401k) and then have to cut back your life when you retire. It doesn't matter if you earn $2,000 or $20,000 a month. If you follow the conventional theories chances are you will be broke when you retire.

It is not what you make; it is what you do outside of your job

What you have to realize is that your job alone will not accomplish retiring young, quitting your job, and having a lot of money. You will need to look beyond your job for additional ways to make money and particularly for your Forever Cash investments.

And you don't have to be wealthy to do this. You can, just like I did, start wherever you are (in my case with $3500 in the bank and a bunch of debt) and become financially independent and secure in three to five years, and truly wealthy a couple of years after that.

Wealth through Forever Cash is a proven path that the vast majority of people who created generational wealth or "old money" (wealth that may have been created fast but then lasted for generations) have applied and lived by. If you fully engage and fully understand the concepts, I believe it will change your way of thinking about money and it will change the way you use money- forever.

And when you apply the principles diligently, it is my conviction that you cannot go down any other path but the one leading to financial success and everlasting wealth- for you and for the people coming after you. Why is that so important?

Sometimes, I like to use my imagination and fast forward into the future ... to see the end my life. I imagine I am lying on my deathbed and taking my final breaths. Holding my hand will be my family. As I imagine myself taking those final breaths, I wonder what my final thoughts will be. When I reflect on the life that I have lived, what will be my greatest triumphs, and what will be my most bitter regrets? What will be the lingering "what ifs" of my life?

I don't look at this mental exercise as too macabre; instead, I look at it as a way to help me set my priorities now, while I can still determine the direction of my life. When I look back on the life that I have led, I don't want to think about "what could have been" or about the missed opportunities. I want to be able to think about all the good I have accomplished and the reputation that I have left behind. Most importantly, I want to think about the people that I have helped, especially my wife and daughter.

At the time of this writing, my daughter is only six years old. When I leave this world (which I don't plan to do for a long time), I want to know I have left behind something of great value for her. While I do plan to leave her something financially, more than anything I hope to leave her with a financial education, a way of looking at money that will help her throughout her life. You see, I will never push my daughter to get a high-paying job, like being a doctor or a CEO of a billion-dollar company, to guarantee her economic security.

Instead, I want to help my daughter take care of her finances so that she can spend her time doing whatever she wants, whatever she loves to do. If she wants to, she can spend her days playing the piano, painting, or even being a doctor or a CEO, if that's what she wants to do, as long as she knows how to make money outside of what she does "for a living." If I have given her that before I find myself on my deathbed, then I can die a happy man.

I want to repeat that because it's so important.

The money thing is not what you do in your job. Instead, what you *want* to do is to *learn* the money thing, so that as a result of having mastered money, you can spend your life doing what you want, no matter what that is. When you know how money works and how you can make money irrespective of what you do from 9–5, then you can choose to do whatever you want from 9-5. When you do that, you will always know that whatever you do you don't do it for the money, but out of love for it.

Until you get to that place, you might want to turn things around and, instead of quitting your job so that you can get wealthy, you must *use* your job to become wealthy and to fund your quest to get out of the hamster wheel of earn-to-spend.

Chapter 5

STOP LISTENING TO BAD ADVICE!

In the previous chapter, I talked about the three different kinds of cash and how most people, the ones who are not generationally wealthy, mostly work for One-Time Cash and don't even know or see that there are other kinds of cash.

There is a reason that this is not public knowledge.

The reason is that much of the financial world has the incentive to keep you financially uneducated and dependent. As Charlie Munger, Warren Buffett's long-time business partner, wrote in his excellent speech titled "On the Psychology of Human Misjudgment," the most underestimated human power is the power of incentives. People act based on incentives and will do way more than you think just to get an incentive. You can read the entire interview/speech at www.ForeverCash. com/munger.

What is going on in the world does, truly, border on brainwash. You can't turn the TV on and watch anything having to do with the finances, or open a news or financial magazine without being bombarded with advertising of slightly silver-haired men lounging around a pool or the beach with their grandchildren. The advertisement inevitably reads: "If you want to retire in peace, call us—[phone number]. XYZ Financial Management team stands by your side to help you enjoy the retirement you deserve …" While the advertising itself would be fine if the product would deliver, the problem is that the advice given by the financial industry just does not work.

I wanted to dedicate an entire chapter of this book to show you— hopefully— just how strong the incentives are to keep you financially in the dark so that at the end, *you* hopefully will be able to stop listening to the bad financial advice offered by the vast majority of "experts" out there or at least be able to pick one of the few good advisors from the masses of bad ones.

You must take charge of your life, because —truly —your life depends on it. You can't afford to outsource your financial life.

I must explain that I do believe that most financial experts—and that includes financial brokers, planners—are probably convinced that their advice will actually help their clients retire in safety. If you look deeply enough, you will even find some truly good financial advisors out there who have *your* wealth at heart. But whether they are in their heart good, in many cases, what you are ultimately being offered as an investment vehicle is a matter of what their incentives are and, in most cases, these incentives are set up against you.

Most of the financial instruments you are being recommended, while having some benefits for you, are designed and created to benefit mostly one party, the one who sells them to you. While the industry tells you otherwise, the odds are stacked against you to make money through the use of traditional financial advice.

A financial advisor, in theory, has one main job: His job should be to help you protect and increase your hard-earned money. But his true *reasons* for selling you his financial instruments like annuities, wholesale life insurance, mutual funds, and so on, are that he (or she) has to put food on his family's table. So the fact that those financial advisors get a commission for every investment they sell to you, combined with the fact that some investments pay the advisor higher commissions than others, should already show you that there is an inherent conflict of interest and calls into question if their advice is always in your best interest.

There is even an insider joke in the financial planning industry where the planner says: "I made money; the firm made money. Well, two out of three ain't bad." This joke indicates that the third person—the *customer*—didn't make any money in the deal. That is the reality of the regular financial advice world.

Here is how it works.

There are three ways that the financial advice industry is being paid:

- **Advisor Type 1:** Via commission for the products they sell to you. The vast majority, including the big firms.
- **Advisor Type 2:** Fee-based advisor whom you pay a flat fee per year to advise you and to manage your finances.
- **Advisor Type 3:** Percentage-based advisor whom you pay a small percentage of your overall invested assets under his/her management.

Advisor Type 2 and Advisor Type 3 are actually good because their interest is either neutral or positively aligned with yours. If you pay someone an annual fee, you will make sure he or she makes your assets perform well enough to be worth that fee. If you pay someone a small percentage (like 1 percent) of the asset value under management by this person, then his incentives are aligned with yours to make your assets grow as quickly as possible and avoid losing money. Losing money for you means he, too, will take a pay cut, and making money means he will get a raise and, perhaps, you even give him more money to manage.

Unfortunately, most financial advice is product based and the advisor gets a commission for each product you end up buying based on his/her recommendation.

And while there are some truly good exceptions who want you to be happy (they don't want you to leave and take your money elsewhere) and who are crushed if you, for some reason, end up losing money based on their advice, he also needs to feed his own family and, therefore, he is tempted to sell what maximizes his commissions.

Every time you listen to their advice and, as a result, you move money from one fund to another, they get paid. Every time you buy some whole life insurance from your financial planners, they get a nice commission on that sale. Did you know that whole life insurance pays some of the highest commissions paid anywhere? No wonder one of the highest-sold products out there is whole life insurance. That is no coincidence, yet this is one kind of insurance that has fairly high fees, and where you pay (it pulls money out of your pocket) for decades, before you start seeing anything. The only thing "whole life" in "whole life insurance" is the commission that goes to the advisor for his or her whole life. *But not to you.* In my book, that is *not* a good asset. I like assets that make me money from the day I purchase them, not something I have to pay for decades only to then get my money back slowly and with a terrible interest rate. Now I am not saying that life insurance is bad. There is a place for this type of financial instrument, but you have to know how much you need and when you are overinsured.

As a matter of fact, this is what happened to my friend. His advisor for years and years pushed only whole life insurance and he, not knowing that this was bad advice, listened and bought a huge amount of whole life insurance. He literally was paying thousands of dollars a month just for that kind of insurance until he decided to have his insurance needs checked by someone else whose incentive structure was more aligned with his. The result was that he immediately switched advisors, cancelled 75 percent of all his whole life insurance and instead uses that money to invest in other things that grow faster and provide growth and cash flow *right away*. He is happier, has more money, and still carries adequate insurance in case of death.

Can you imagine your financial advisor or broker telling you to invest in real estate or to buy and hold a dividend-paying stock? It doesn't happen often because the financial planner would lose. It would be like a car dealership telling you to keep your old car and not buy a new one. At the end of the day, most financial brokerages and planners, while they may be often sincere and want to help your investment grow, will often—all other things being the same —recommend the methods that will make them a higher commission, *even if it comes at your expense*.

The entire financial advisor industry actually benefits from keeping their clients (you) in the dark, keeping you uneducated, and keeping you dependent on their "professional advice" for guidance. Financial management companies want you to give them your hard-earned money month after month without ever asking if there is a better way to make it grow, or without ever wondering if you are capable of choosing your own investments. They even offer electronic withdrawal of your bank account, and they work with your employer to offer "companywide 401ks and IRAs that you can automatically contribute to." On a national scale, the banking industry, the mutual fund industry, and the investment advice industry spends millions, lobbying for the creation of certain laws to benefit themselves and their way of doing things. In fact, they spend a huge amount of money trying to accomplish these goals. One of their favorite outlets for influence is the media.

Also, advisors and financial brokers want you only to invest in the stock market, but nobody tells you it might take twelve years for losses in the stock market to be recovered, as it happened from 2001 to 2013, which now is commonly called the "lost decade." And that while you receive no cash flow from the stock you earn. That fact is conveniently ignored and, if asked about, your question is only answered in general statements like "on average, the stock market over the last 100 years has outperformed other asset classes." But that answer is not helpful if you happen to be the unlucky person who has to start drawing from your amount of money during a time when the stock market is down, and your savings are diminished.

If you do need financial advice and want to have some money/ investments in financial instruments, I would at least ask you to work with the ones who have their interests aligned with yours. I recommend you go to www.ForeverCash.com/advisors for more details on the person or style I feel comfortable recommending.

But remember, most wealthy people didn't make their money in the stock market; they just keep some of their money in the stock market.

If you choose the stock market as your vehicle to financial freedom, consider educating yourself on what a good investment is and what a good investment is not—and how you can make extra money in the stock market. For example, there are fairly conservative options-investing strategies (using straddles, or long-term puts and calls; or selling short-term, out-of-the-money options) that allow you to limit risks and still make money in the stock market on a reliable basis. If this doesn't mean anything to you, you might start to understand why you are not making as much money as you could. Because some of these option trading techniques have great potential to make you quite predictable cash of several thousand dollars a month—if you do it right.

If you truly want to get financially independent, you must follow an alternative path, and I have yet to find one that has a better track record than investments in Forever Cash Assets.

Just be aware that when you head down this new path toward Forever Cash, you will get weird looks from the people you hang out with. They don't know what you know, and you know that they are still dialed into the conventional wisdom and following the crowd and … staying broke. Some of them will actually even try to hold you back and try to tell you that "investing is risky," but if you are prepared and have the education to invest properly, you know that it is staying on the old path of 401k, forty years of work for two weeks' vacation that is risky. It is risky to your health, to your spirit, and of course to your ability to retire in decency—let alone style—any time in your life.

I strongly believe in the following two sayings:

- *It is none of your business what people think of you.*
- *Your neighbors or other people don't pay your bills.*

In other words, what do you care what "they" think about you?

I like these sayings because of the message they transmit. You and you alone—nobody else—is responsible for making things happen. Nobody else is in charge of making the money to pay the bills other than you. So, it won't help your financial situation a bit if you don't do something because of "what the neighbors will think." Who cares what the neighbors think? They are not going to be pitching in to pay for your retirement.

Since you can't control what people think all day long anyway, why fuss about what they think of you? Live your own life. Do what you have to do to take care of your family, and allow the world around you to do and think whatever they want.

Those are two of my premises in life.

While my beliefs may sound harsh, I think people are way too concerned about what people around them think; that is, until they realize people around them don't think about them at all. There is a saying that I heard and which I have found to be true:

When you are twenty, you always wonder what people think about you.
When you are forty, you don't care what people think about you.
When you are sixty, you realize that everyone is just busy thinking about themselves and not about you.

While I agree that the narcissist in each of us wants for people to think about us, and they certainly do sometimes, the fact is that people are busy with their own lives. Just tell me when is the last time you thought seriously about your neighbor, or the people at your church, or at your country club ... other than when you were about to go to meet them. And if you did for how long was it before you switched over to thinking about yourself and your own challenges in life again? You see, we *are* busy with our own lives.

So then, why worry about conversations that neighbors or coworkers might have about your life decisions that they probably don't even have and are just happening in your imagination? Part of breaking through is breaking the cage of peer pressure and social conformity that holds us back and forces us into making certain decisions "because that's the way things are done."

Anytime I feel that I am being peer pressured into something or that I need to keep up with the Joneses (and yes it even happens to me—I am not immune), I remember that by not paying my bills, they make it clear that they are not responsible for making sure I can retire in style. The same is true for you. *You and you alone are responsible for your financial future.* That usually should take the pressure off and allow you to make a rational decision that is better for you and your family's future.

Again, don't give up the reins of your financial life to anyone else. Don't adjust your life according to what people think about you. Do what you need to do to take care of your family. It is not always easy. You will question yourself when you see that everyone is doing one thing, and you are starting down a path that goes in a different direction. The media pushes against you. The big banks and financial institutions do not want you to think. They just want you to open your wallet and to give them your money. Behind all the façade that some people put up about how well they are doing, you must wonder how well is what they are doing really working for them. You can't afford to be financially ignorant if you ever want to live in comfort, without any financial worries. Financial education is what makes the difference between struggling each day and knowing that you have enough, even more than enough, to enjoy life. Without financial education and without learning the methods and criteria to tell a good investment from a bad one, you won't know when you are being taken and when to act on a solid opportunity.

Chapter 6

EDUCATION IS GOOD— BUT WHAT KIND?

E ducation is good. It is good in a different way and for different purposes than you might have thought.

College is necessary. It is needed for the advancement of technology, humanity, and to make sure we live like humans. There is no better indicator of societal advancement than the level of education the masses receive.

Look at any third-world country. The way to get that country out of poverty is education, a stable government (something that comes with increased education of the masses), and capitalism in its various forms. Many countries have shown that they could move out of their third-world status. We usually call them "emerging markets," and this includes places like India, Brazil, South Africa, and many others. Poverty is far from being eliminated in those countries, but these countries have taken significant steps in the right direction. A true middle class is growing and can now—for the first time ever—send their kids to good schools, even bilingual schools, so that they can advance to a university level and get better jobs or start businesses. As a result of that, they begin to afford cars, live in decent brick houses with modern plumbing, cook in properly equipped kitchens, and eat healthier foods— all of this allows them to live longer and healthier lives. Plus, they will go on to repeat the same cycle for their kids and their grandchildren. And a great deal of the credit for all this positive change goes to the availability of quality education.

The same is true in the United States, where, according to an article in *The Wall Street Journal* from February 21, 2012, during the last recession more than 50 percent of all high school dropouts over the age of twenty-five were unemployed.[4] That number is usually below 5 percent for college graduates. That provides the predictability that a college degree *does* equal a better life, a better job, and more comfort.

The conventional wisdom that investing in a college education is the best way to guarantee a better financial future is true. However, as you have probably noticed by now, this book is not about living the traditional life—the one where you have a job, avoid being laid off, and fly under the radar for forty years until you can retire.

What's wrong with traditional education?

Here are the issues.

While the first degree often pays off in higher pay and lower unemployment, any additional back-to-school effort is doubtful in its benefits.

Formal education is a conservative defensive play. It teaches you to fill a role as an employee in a system that is designed to keep you mediocre. And it won't teach you anything about money and how to be financially successful in life.

In his book *How Rich People Think,* author Steve Siebold writes, "Average people think the road to riches is paved with formal education. Rich people believe in acquiring specific knowledge."

Let me ask you: Did you go to college after graduating from high school? If so, what was your motive?

If you were thinking that a college degree makes it easier to get hired and that it will earn you a better salary, then you were correct. I commend you for going to college. The idea that a diploma can affect your livelihood is not a new one. We are all trained to try and increase our value to the world by getting more and more certificates and diplomas. Society has been trained to see college as the solution to all problems that relate to making money. If you need more money or if you are having trouble trying to find a job, what do the experts say? "Go back to school." Were you just laid off after twenty years working for the same firm? "Go back to school." When the United States falls into a recession and unemployment goes up? "Go back to school." And you see it in the numbers. Enrollment in colleges soars when a recession comes in. People think that the added education will get them a better job when they are finished, or they think it will mask their unemployment for a while. *Officially*, they can say they were not unemployed; they just decided to go back to school.

Going back to school, I dare to say, doesn't necessarily work out financially unless you enroll in one of the few guaranteed high-paying professions like, perhaps, one of the medical specialties. But that certainly takes more than two years to accomplish.

Think about it. Getting out of the workforce for two years and missing out on the salary to get a master's degree and spending anywhere from $30,000 to $70,000 (or more) for school tuition and living expenses may end up costing you easily a truer real loss of $100,000 in actual money spent and missed earnings while you were out of the workforce. That does not even take into consideration the interest accruing on those student loans once you are finished. Afterward, if that gets you a job making $10,000 (pre-tax) more per year, you will have to work for anywhere from fifteen to twenty years to just break even after all those expenses.

Believe me, I am not against education. I have a bachelor's degree and two master's degrees from good schools. My wife has a bachelor's degree and her master's degree is from a top school. I spent a full seven years in college; Michelle spent five. We believe that college has its place. Michelle and I are putting a great deal of emphasis on getting my daughter a formal education in the best schools available. I hope my daughter will go to one of the best colleges in the world. I want her to go there to ensure that she grows up to be a well-adjusted and well-rounded individual. We want her to learn about many different subjects, to meet people from around the world, and to grow as a human being.

Yes, this has nothing to do with her education about how to be financially successful. I have absolutely no illusion that she will learn the slightest thing about that in college. How to make money is *my* responsibility to teach her. I will teach her that outside of the traditional classroom setting in the school of life. I will take her along to my tenants and show her how she can use her *mind* to make more money instead of her time and hands. I will teach her to start her own money-making venture as soon as she is able to do simple addition and multiplication.

So you need an idea about what to go to college for. Most people either never turn their brain on, or they just accept the conventional wisdom that going back to school will help you get a higher-paying job, without running the numbers, or they have wrong expectations of what a bit or a lot more college can do for them.

College is great for any profession that you plainly can't do without having experienced a higher level of education. I wouldn't, for example, want to go into surgery with a doctor who didn't go to college and medical school and had not been trained for years. I would also not want to be defended by a lawyer who has not gone through law school. I want a lawyer who knows how to read the law, how to interpret the law, and how to work in the U.S. legal system. Professions like these allow the people holding these diplomas to start their own businesses and perform their learned trade, if it is desired or required. They may also make a substantial amount of money if they are good at what they do.

Just going back to college after you already have a degree or for a second degree because people told you to do that doesn't make sense to me. Many people, after they graduate from college, end up working in a field that is totally different from what they went to college for or in a field where they don't need a college degree in the first place. So if many people work in a field that either requires no college degree or apparently not the one they went to school for, the question arises of what college is good for.

So what *is* college good for?

Other than spending four years having a great time and partying, you should spend that time learning how to learn. Through case studies and independent learning, you learn to *find* the information you are looking for to make your case. That is actually a skill that can help you in any aspect of life whether it is as an employee or as a business owner. Being resourceful in finding information is a valuable resource to have.

When you are on a campus, you learn to start living on your own. You learn how to become a responsible adult. By interacting with others and forging new friendships, you learn new social skills and make friends that will, hopefully, last a lifetime. But, in most cases, it will *not* get you closer to financial freedom.

And while in college you learn either technical or tactical skills that help you do a job.

But here is the biggest problem with a college education:

No matter what you go to college for, you won't learn to be financially independent, and you won't learn how to make money. Even medical doctors are being sent out to start their own practices without having more than a few hours of instructions on how to actually run their practice so that they can enjoy it and make money in the process. As a result, there are quite a few medical doctors whose practices don't make it in the market economy.

In college, you won't learn money management, financial freedom, financial intelligence, and business savvy. What you do learn is how to become a highly functional "ant" in the job-based economy of the western world. All those degrees that my wife and I have haven't brought us close to financially being set, safe, and worry free. Not at all. During my years of schooling, I learned about many subjects. Even if they were applicable to the business world, it was taught from the point of view of preparing us to work as a little soldier in a multinational company. We learned about finance in theoretical concepts that had absolutely no application to making money for ourselves. We were taught about micro- and macroeconomic concepts of how national economies compete against each other. With all that, however, we did not learn much at all about how we could take these concepts and make money with them on our own.

I mean, how *would* we have learned anything about that? The professors we had were mainly career professors who worked for a salary and were trying to reach tenure. Many had never worked in any larger company themselves, had never run a company themselves, and had never had to make money outside the ivory towers of their campuses. They were highly intelligent people, but people who lived largely in their own heads, with no application and knowledge of how life out in the real world happened.

If you were to throw them out in the streets where they would have to fend for themselves, many would struggle. So when you look at it that way, you can see that it is not an environment to learn how to be financially secure. Sure, these schools taught me all I needed to know to get a good job with good benefits, and they even offered classes on how to put together a great resume and how to behave during an interview—but they did not even try to teach us how to apply the business administration knowledge for the benefit of our *own* business. For that matter, not a single one of any of the three schools I attended even offered any classes on entrepreneurism. *Nothing.* I understand that has changed now a bit. Some colleges offer entrepreneur classes, and I applaud that, but there is still a way to go.

That's why I say that school is the worst place to go to learn how to make money. They don't teach you what you need to know about that subject.

It's the *type* of education that you need that makes the difference. You need education that you can actually apply, that helps you succeed in life—particularly financially. You need an education that teaches you how to deal with money. I'm not talking about just any type of education; I am speaking of a specific kind of education.

If you want to be financially successful, you must learn:

- How to invest
- How to tell a good investment from a bad one
- How to make more money in your life in—and outside of—your job
- How to find ways to invest in the stock market without the risk of losing money (there are strategies for that)
- How to outsource cheaply the things in life you don't enjoy so that you can spend more time on doing the things you do enjoy and which bring you forward personally *and* financially
- How to get more than the 1–2 percent that banks offer on your deposits in a safe way. For example, there are ways to get 12–36 percent on your money in government-guaranteed investments, like tax liens
- How to find cash flow investments that will give you Forever Cash for, well, ever!

If you are the entrepreneurial type and want to start a full-blown business, you also need to educate yourself on:

- How to manage a business by the numbers
- How to hire the right people
- How to run businesses remotely without having to be there every day or even without having to live close by
- How to do marketing for your company

- How to find opportunities at every corner and how to tell which opportunity is a good one
- How to keep your cost under control
- How to have a strategy that works for your business and how to implement that strategy

When you have that kind of education, even just the first part of the list I just gave you, you are prepared to take advantage of opportunities when they present themselves. Unfortunately, this kind of knowledge is not being taught in a "regular" college. But you *can* find it. You *can* learn it. To get a set of free videos with more information on that subject, go to www.ForeverCash.com/education. I have a great deal of free information there, and even a discussion forum where you and I can discuss these subjects in detail.

Once you do get that kind of knowledge and real-life education, you will never again be worried about not having enough money. With the knowledge of how to make money independent of a job, you will always be able to have food on the table for you and your family.

So how do you get it?

When I see someone who has exactly the kind of life, business, and income that I want for myself, here is what I do.

I find the best person I can find on that subject. This means I'm looking for the one with the most *real-life* experience, and I commit to learning from them.

Sometimes, I have to pay to meet these people. This is particularly true if they are playing life and business on a much higher level than I am, but I am willing to pay for that experience because their time is valuable, very valuable. There are many knowledgeable people out there who are willing to teach you what they know.

I also join organizations or groups where these people are members so I can be closer to them.

I read anything and everything I can about that subject and about what sets the successful people in that industry apart from the rest.

I take action then, and I begin to implement what I have learned.

In summary, I think you now understand that learning and education are important. College is just *one* place for education, and the kind of education you get there is mostly only good in the job world. The kind of knowledge to be financially independent and have Forever Cash come into your life is being taught in real time in the real world. That's why learning is not over when you leave school. It is a different kind of learning, a kind of learning that you need to do outside of school.

Stop thinking you are finished learning once you leave school.

When we talk about learning or about getting an education, where does your mind go? Does it take you back to those days of sitting in a classroom, listening to a teacher ramble on and on about something that you care nothing about? For most kids, all they can think about is how much longer they have to wait until the bell rings. When they are older, they can't wait to graduate and to find a job. Then, the learning will be over, and they can finally start living their life. Did you feel that way when you were younger? Do you feel you are all finished with your learning? Did you put your books in a box or perhaps even burn them because you were exhilarated that, now that you have that degree, you no longer need to study?

I did the same thing, and isn't that what most people do? They finish their education and then never open any books again.

That is a mistake.

What I did not realize was that when you get out of school your *mandatory* learning ends. Your *personal* education is just getting started.

When I was finally finished with college, I entered the job world. I was never against hard work and whatever I did, I did full tilt. But I also never had the desire to spend my life in an office with people I didn't know, some of whom I didn't like, and none of which I would have probably spent much time with if I had met them under different circumstances. When I left college, I *finally* felt like I didn't have to read whatever the teacher/professor had selected for me. *Finally*, I could just go to work, come home, *turn my brain off,* and just relax with my wife and watch TV or go out with friends. I could afford to do it, or so I thought. After all, I was following the conventional wisdom and advice, putting 10 percent of my salary away into a 401k and was doing all the things the world was telling me to do.

Are you ready for some frightening statistics? Despite the financial gospel that is preached across the country, most Americans aren't ready to retire. They have been told to save until they reach a certain figure, but they are nowhere near it. Some 75 percent of Americans who are nearing retirement age had less than $30,000 in their retirement accounts in 2010. Look at your expenses: How long would it take you to spend $30,000? That's not all. For the poorest Americans, in the 50-to-64 age bracket, the average amount saved for retirement was $16,034.[5]

The Baby Boomers are reevaluating retirement and their decision on how and when to retire. Officially, they are saying they want to stay active and to keep feeling useful. While that is certainly the case for some of them, I don't buy it. I don't buy that anyone who is seventy years old, who takes a host of different pills a day for various ailments, and who has not yet seen the world would rather work as a waiter or waitress in a diner, or at Wal-Mart as a greeter, or even in a back office doing accounting. I can't believe they wouldn't rather travel the world, stay in luxury hotels, take cruises, and go visit their grandkids. The statement that "we want to stay active" is, for many, just a lie that they are saying to keep face.

This goes to another deep belief average people have about money, which is completely different from the wealthy, as reported by Steve Siebold in his book, *How Rich People Think*. Average people let money stress them out. Rich people find peace of mind in wealth.

These people don't want to have to publicly admit either that their financial plans for retirement either never existed or that they have failed miserably. It is painful to admit that you followed the wrong path. The worst part is that many people even at that stage don't realize that they were on the wrong path, and, as a result, they go back to the same financial advice that put them on that path in the first place to get more advice.

They have just stopped learning; they stopped using their brains. Instead of turning into a mindless robot that just sits on the couch and turns the TV on when the 5 o'clock whistle blows, I believe in scheduling "thinking time." Most people walk through the day not ever thinking an original thought all day. They just pass the day on autopilot going through the same nonproductive repetitive thoughts about what they should eat or what the neighbors might say, that they have to wash the car, get groceries, and call their buddies. Although these are, of course, thoughts, they are not critical-thinking thoughts. They are not thoughts that will help you break through and find new ways to solve a problem.

Bill Gates Sr. wrote in his book, *Showing Up for Life,* that when Bill Gates III, his son, was about nine years old, his parents and siblings all were in the car waiting for him to come out of the house. When he finally showed up, his mom would ask: "Bill, where were you?" He would answer: "I was thinking, Mom. Don't you guys ever just think?"

Bill Gates, the founder of Microsoft, is today one of the richest men on Earth. I don't think that's a coincidence.

The truth about learning after school is over is that this is the time when you get to learn what you want to learn and when you want to learn it. Instead of shutting off your brain, it is time to ask it to work on what you think is important. Your financial life is one of the most important parts of your life you can ask your brain to work on. Use it, and use the time you have outside of work to apply your brain to advance in life.

Let me finish this chapter with a story about how turning on your brain and learning in the real world can make a huge difference. This story is about Dustin Matthews, a friend of mine from Tampa, Florida, and what he has accomplished. What he did brought him from the bottom of the corporate food chain to becoming the CEO of a seven-figure-per-year company. He knew he wanted to learn about marketing. So, after graduating from college, instead of looking for a dead-end job with benefits, he approached an Internet marketing and training company in his hometown and offered to work for free for them. Yes, you read that correctly. He offered to work for *free*. Needless to say, the company accepted his offer. He not only worked for free but he came in early, stayed late, and absorbed every piece of marketing he could learn.

Fast forward a few years. He and the founder of the original company where he went to work for free, partnered up in a new venture and he is a 50 percent partner and the CEO of that company. Their expertise is marketing, and they now charge up to $15,000 a *day* for their expertise. And you know what? They are booked 200 days of the year.

While I understand that not many people who are in the position to work want to work for free, perhaps having to move back home to live with their parents so they can work for free without going broke, it does show what a difference being a little creative, along with some active thinking and a willingness to learn in the real world, can make. First, he was willing to give, and then he was willing to receive. That is a characteristic of many successful people, too. They first gave their time or expertise, and then they made money when their time or expertise produced results.

Perhaps you should examine what you went to college for, and see if you cannot, in fact, get something positive out of it. Look to see if you can find a way to use that knowledge to make extra money, outside of your primary job. After all, most people work in areas that are different from what they went to college for. Your college degree is probably not being used right now. Put it to use. Think creatively about what you could do to make use of it in a way that can make you some money. Use Dustin's example to make you think outside that box. You will come up with something that helps you break out of where you are now.

Chapter 7

BREAKING THE
HAMSTER WHEEL

Have you ever seen a hamster running on the little wheel in his cage? Those little creatures put all their energy and concentration into pumping those little legs just as quickly as they can. They are rewarded by watching that wheel spin and spin, even though they don't move a single inch. The faster they run, the faster the wheel spins, but they don't accomplish anything.

For most people, life is a hamster wheel of financial hell. They get older, they make more money, they buy more stuff, they get into more debt, and they become more dependent on a high-paying job. Soon enough, married with two kids, they can't afford to let go of that job, and although they might not like what they do day in and day out, they don't see a way out. They are trapped and are running faster by the day getting nowhere; they think this is normal.

This is how life goes for most people:

- They earn money at a full-time job.
- They spend that money for stuff.
- They get a raise and earn more money.
- They raise their living expenses and spend more money. They buy that new car or house and commit to more monthly expenses for years to come.
- Then cash is just as tight as it was before, only at a higher level of material comfort, now that there is a higher level of living and more expenses.
- They either work harder to get another promotion or they go back to school (and spend a lot of money doing that) to get a better job to be able to earn more money.
- They earn more money so they can spend more and raise their living expenses even more.
- Repeat.

Around and around it goes. This hamster wheel of financial hell can spin faster, but—at the end of the day—what has changed? Is there more money in the bank? Is the future less frightening? Is there greater financial security? Not at all. The shocking thing that I have seen is that this cycle is the same for everyone, no matter what their income is.

Truly generationally wealthy people consider cash flow to be the fountain of their wealth. They only spend the interest (and, ideally, only a part of the interest) their investments made—the interest that comes in without their working much (or at all) for that income.

Most people— even the vast majority of the high rollers you see living the large life, driving the big cars and living in the mansions—violate that rule. However, the ones who get it are the ones living the truly wealthy lives. They also drive the same big cars, live in the same large houses, but they didn't slay the golden goose to pay for their toys. Instead their cars, vacations, and houses are being paid with the cash these proverbial golden goose investments throw off.

That is a material difference, a significant difference. If you *get* this difference, your life should take on a new quality. If you don't, then let me tell you again.

The truly wealthy have their investments pay for their lifestyle, not their active income. And if they had a job when they started their journey, they made their money mostly outside their job.

Open your eyes to this. I hope you will understand that it is *this method* that will allow you to retire early and in style and *never* have to worry about money again.

It took us ten months to step out of the hamster wheel. You, too, can reach this, no matter where you are right now. It might take you less time than it took me, or it might take you longer. That depends on you, but what I do know is that if you follow the steps—which I call the Wealth Wheel® process—and focus on Forever Cash investments, you cannot fail. You will be out of the hamster wheel of earn-to-spend faster, living in more comfort than you ever could if you followed the traditional advice.

The way to *lasting* financial independence is to create a life where you have enough Temporary and Forever Cash Flow from assets coming in that you don't *need* to work anymore—or if you love what you do, so that you can dedicate your life to your calling, your mission, and your life's purpose without having to worry about financial matters.

When you reached the level of Temporary Cash and Forever Cash income, you will be able to either:

- Quit your job (retire) at the same financial level you are now living at
- Quit your job and use the free time to build more wealth faster
- Keep going for another few years to build more and more abundance to live in luxury forever

Understanding the importance of Forever Cash Flow freedom is an important part of your financial education. However, it is also important to look at the bad example of others and learn from their mistakes. Let's take a moment and see why so many people have trouble in their finances. It starts with the way people view money.

They equate their financial health and future prospects with the size of the paycheck from their job/position/company performance. While people of all income brackets, even the high earners, and even company owners might save some of the money (maybe to put it into savings and stocks or whole life insurance policies), most of them never even once think about being able to use that excess money today, now, to create a second stream of *cash flow* that supports them, backs them, and ultimately guarantees them a retirement in luxury—even if their high income job disappears, even if their company goes under, or even if they simply aren't able to sell their company for as much as they thought they would be able to.

There are many stories about people who have lost companies due to bad management or due to a recession or a shift in the market. They certainly didn't plan for this and never followed the process to secure a safe retirement for them and their loved ones forever, no matter what happens to the company.

If only these people had known how easy it was, they would have been able to divert some of the profits they made from their job or business into another path, a path that would have secured their livelihood and their financial security (at a high level) as well as that of their heirs for many generations. But most people just don't think that way and, instead, fall into the trap of focusing on making money and spending money.

Even if they drive Porsches and live in mansions, the trap of earning to spend is the fast lane to staying broke. They are still broke, only on a higher level of comfort.

Look at some examples: actor Nicolas Cage, boxers Evander Holyfield and Mike Tyson, basketball players Scottie Pippen and Dennis Rodman, rapper MC Hammer, baseball player Curt Schilling, and many others. They all made huge amounts of money during their careers. Yet each one of them lost it all! Why?

I have always wondered why there are so many people who make a huge amount of money one time in their lives and then lose it all. Athletes and actors aren't the only ones; your everyday higher-income earner, and even the middle class American, have been known to do the same thing again and again and again. They are the people who come up to me at my seminars and tell me about having—at one time— hundreds of thousands or even millions of dollars of net worth, only to lose it all and soon find themselves unable to retire and worried about losing their house.

I have learned that there are many reasons for this phenomenon. One of them, of course, is a simple lack of financial understanding. By just handing their money over to someone (who may be up to no good), many high earners have watched their money disappear into a cloud of legal fees, bad investments, and outright theft. They blow their money on things they didn't need but only *felt* they needed, based out of a deep feeling of insecurity and of having to please the people around them.

Most importantly, these people lost the huge amounts of money that they had earned or had been given because they just didn't know that there were other alternatives around for them to use that would have ensured abundant wealth forever.

You see, they never learned the missing steps. It's like they had all the tools to build a great wealth fortress but no knowledge how to build it.

I can help you build that fortress. As I described before, the missing step is to learn to use your income differently: Instead of making money to spend it, you can convert actual cash into a fountain of money that runs forever. Use your money to *invest* it into Forever Cash Assets that spit out cash flow—*forever.*

This is how the wealthy European aristocrats and the families which have been wealthy for generations in the United States still generate their income today. In Germany, where I am from, there is still a lot of "old money" in the hands of the ancient, aristocratic families. They have lost most of their political power, but they still own the assets that originally gave it to them, and they know how to live off of those assets, cultivate them, and pass them on from one generation to the next—all without paying much in taxes, and often all without having to trade their time (at a job) for money—*ever.* Can you imagine that there are people who are living off the twenty-fifth generation of the cash flow thrown off from assets created in the sixteenth century, or—in some cases—even earlier than that? That is the reality of what *you* can create if you just learn how and even if you start with almost nothing right now.

Once you understand the process, it's just a matter of following it for a little while. Things will speed up beyond your imagination.

Even if you don't care too much about what your heirs do once you leave this Earth, how they will fare in life, the application of these principles—if applied diligently—can put *you,* within just a few years, into a position where you won't have to work anymore and can just live off the cash flow you created.

For as long as you keep things going, following this method will make you wealthier as time goes by and allow you to live better and, if you want to, in more and more luxury without ever having to touch the underlying assets you have created. You will then have the opportunity to decide if you want to pass those cash-flow-generating assets on to your heirs, give them to charity, or at the end of your life, just liquidate them and blow the money to go out with a bang! It will be up to you.

You are probably thinking: "Well, Jack, I see what you're saying, but I don't have $50 million dollars to blow! I only have a regular house, a family to feed, a bunch of debt, lots of expenses, and a job that I might—or might not—have next year. How does this story about rich people blowing their savings relate to me?"

I hear and understand where you're coming from. It looks like we're trying to compare apples and oranges. But the lessons rich people have learned still relate to you in a big way. For starters, think about your goals of perhaps retiring and quitting your job early. Because you need much less money per month than a celebrity, you need to invest less and you need to do this whole process on a much lower financial level than the high earners who *need* to replace a lot of income.

In a sense, it is easier if you make less money now, because it takes less to replace your current income.

Cash flow is the solution. *Better* than that, however, is Forever Cash.

Instead of thinking about making a pile of money, think about this: How much money would you need to have coming in *each month* to live the way you want? That's how you need to start thinking. When you focus on cash flow, it doesn't leave you at the mercy of the financial system the financial industry pitches. Cash flow doesn't necessarily depend on the value of the underlying asset.

When you learn to think in terms of Forever Cash Flow, your world will change. You will no longer want to go and spend your hard-earned money instantly on things you don't need and which lose value. Instead, you will want to invest it in something that brings you cash flow forever, and then, if you still want the "stuff," use that money on toys. You then use Forever Cash for personal expenses and not One-Time Cash. And if you remember, Forever Cash replenishes itself again and again even after the item you bought with the money from the Forever Cash Flow is worthless. Yet, if you use One-Time Cash, the money is gone, and the item you bought is worthless, broken, or lost.

Most people just accept the conventional wisdom. You see your neighbors having three cars with matching payments on them and a large mortgage, and it becomes normal. If all the people around you work to spend, it's normal. If everyone around you has jobs and lives the 40/5/2 lifestyle (forty years' work, five days a week, with two days off on the weekend), it seems normal to you. If anyone you ask puts a few percent into a 401k, and you know of no other way to plan for retirement, then that will seem normal to you.

Most people just never even turn on their brain and start thinking and challenging the conventional wisdom. So even if you are starting at *zero* right now, start by turning on your brain and start thinking.

Here is how you start. You ask yourself questions like:

- How can I use the money that I currently make, whether from my job, from additional income sources, or from both?
- How can I convert some of the savings I might have right now into additional cash flow streams?
- How then can I take the additional cash flow streams and turn them into even more cash flow streams?

Even if you have almost no money right now, but you might have some extra time, ask yourself:

- How can I use that extra time to generate more money (and then go back to the first question)?

If you need $10,000 a month to continue living your current lifestyle, you need to focus on something like twenty assets that produce $500 a month each. Or ten assets that produce $1,000 a month, or two that each produce $5,000 a month.

Buy your first asset for a small amount of money and then build your way up. See? You don't need $2 million, $5 million, or $10 million to retire in comfort. What you need is $4,000, or $5,000, or $10,000, or $20,000 per month of Forever Cash that pays your bills.

That is the path to predictable, achievable, stable, and long-lasting wealth. By going down that path, like the wealthy European aristocrats and the wealthy American families, you can generate more cash flow coming in than you ever thought possible.

I put this newfound knowledge to work in my life. Today, my investments provide the money to pay for most of my lifestyle as well as all of my toys. I focus on finding assets and creating cash flow streams, because I know that once these cash flow streams are big enough and are set up to spit out money every month forever, I can use that cash flow to buy any toy I want and will never have to worry about running out of money. After a few years, when the toy is paid for, and has lost most of its value, the cash flow stream will still be there coming in—month after month after month! I will not have exchanged my time for the toy, and neither will I have had to sell the asset (a house, the dividend stock, the company) to buy that toy. I got to do both, have my cake and eat it; and you can too.

That is the true secret of the rich!

Once the cash-flow sources are spitting cash out, the rich often only spend a (small) portion of their days managing the assets that have built up this optimal cash flow. They take the rest of the day off, play golf, and live *well* using that cash flow. Or if they *choose* to (and "choose" is the key word) spend the rest of the day creating more cash flow, they increase their wealth even more. If the economy crashes, they often don't care because their cash flow keeps coming in despite what the economy is doing.

It's not only the old aristocrats who have understood that. People like Warren Buffett have, too. Think about him. He almost never sells a stock, *loves* investments that bring him dividends, buys companies with large cash flow, and almost always goes against the grain of conventional wisdom. As a result, he is one of the richest men in the world.

It's not that difficult to generate $1 million. I have done it many times. What is more difficult, though, is to *keep* that million dollars and not to just go out and spend it. The Bentleys and the Ferraris and the mansions for sale out there look awfully good when you first have that chunk of change in your pocket. That is where many people (including the famous stars I mentioned earlier) fail. Even normal people give in to temptation. We can go out and buy stuff with the money we earned because we probably never even thought about there being another way. After all, what have we been taught our whole lives? We make money to spend money.

That is why we need to be aware of what's happening. We must be aware of how we are squandering our financial future. We must understand and accept that a plan is necessary—a plan that helps get us in line and keep us in line.

I once had a tenant who—after she dropped her rent check in the mail—called me daily to see if the check had arrived and to see if I could please deposit it quickly. After a while, I asked why she was so eager for me to deposit it. Her answer stunned me. She said, "Well, Jack, I can't stand to see that money in my account. If you don't deposit it quickly, I won't be able to withstand the urge to take it and spend it." I almost fell to the ground laughing, but when I thought about it, I was shocked. This person had so little self-discipline, and her threshold of giving in to temptation was so low that she wouldn't even be able to stay away from the rent money. She was primed to spend any dime she made. It had become second nature to her to make money only for the purpose of spending money. Needless to say that from that day on, I deposited the rent check the day it arrived. I wasn't about to take any chances that my rent check turned into a Gucci bag or a new couch!

Making money to spend money is *the* path to financial ruin.

Instead of going along blindly with what you've been taught, you need to learn to make money to invest it in generating cash flow, and then you can spend the cash flow. I didn't know that when I started, but luckily I figured it out through some serendipitous events and through just plain old trial and error.

Chapter 8

YOUR JOB INCOME HAS NOTHING TO DO WITH YOUR FINANCIAL SUCCESS

T his next statement might conflict with everything you have ever learned.

"Your job income has really *nothing* to do with how financially successful you are in life."

Have you ever heard anyone say, or let alone thought or said one of these things yourself?

Things like:

- "I am making $40,000 in my job, so I can't afford a lot of things."
- Or "I can't make more money because my *job* just doesn't pay more than that."
- Or "I have to just work with what I have and live below my means, because my profession doesn't pay much."
- Or "I love my job, but I have to find another job that pays me more; I just can't live on that salary."

Everyone assumes that your *job* income has to be your only source of income, and if you can't live on that income but love what you do, bad luck. You must either suffer financially and do what you love without getting paid much, or give up what you love and do something else for more pay.

Neither option looks too appealing to me.

The other day, I led a high-level wealth and real estate investing seminar. Once I explained the concepts of Forever Cash and the Wealth Wheel to them, one of the attendees, a wonderful school teacher from Idaho, came up to me during the lunch break and said:

"Jack, I absolutely *love* my job. It is all I ever dreamed about, yet it doesn't pay what I need to be able to retire in style. I have seen my parents retire, lacking a lot of things, and I want to make sure I don't repeat that for myself. So, I need to quit my job and find something else to do that pays more."

After I asked her a few questions, here was my answer: "No, you don't need to quit your job. Your job has nothing to do with how financially successful you are in life."

Luckily, she answered that she already bought three rental houses, each providing a cash flow of $400 a month. She had now run out of money for down payments and figured it would take her decades to build this up to an amount equal to what she was envisioning.

By the end of lunch, we had created a rough blueprint for her on how she can have all the money she wants in just four to five years and can then live the lifestyle she wants to *and* continue to follow her calling of being a teacher. The solution was easy. All she needed to do was to apply some of the things she already knew outside of her job and follow an implementation plan. The system would work for her and bring her about $100,000 to $120,000 in Forever Cash every year just five years from now. It would grow to much more than that if she would continue it for just a few more years. All the while, it would allow her to keep doing what she loves—teaching!

Whenever I tell people that "their job income has nothing to do with how they will fare financially in life," I tend to get blank stares. Yet, people in countries with no social security system to rely on, understand this basic concept. My wife is originally from Honduras, one of the poorest countries in the world with practically no social network to speak of. If you are poor, you better stay healthy; the charity hospitals are horrible. And in spite of—or probably more *because* of—the lack of social services, people understand that they must make sure they can retire (early or late) without relying on the government. One of the preferred ways to do that is to buy a piece of land large enough to have space for three or four small houses. Brick by brick over the years, they build one house cash until they move in. They then start building two to three more little apartments or houses on the same lot. By the time they retire, they have their own house and an additional two to three rental properties, all free and clear, which they can rent out and supplement their pension, if they even have a pension. When they pass away, they pass that real estate on to their kids, who continue to derive the benefits of renting these properties. They choose mainly real estate because that is what is tangible, inflation-proof, and real to them.

Mark Twain said, "Whenever you find yourself on the side of the majority, it's time to pause and reflect." Or in other words, "Conventional wisdom is almost always *wrong*."

It's important to learn to keep your job and your financial future separated from each other. One should not depend on the other. I cannot stress that enough. Let me illustrate that last point with a story from my family.

My grandfather worked as a department store clerk for many years. He never made more than $2,000 a month. In fact, to make things worse, he was a farmer in a German community in former Yugoslavia. When World War II ended, he, my grandmother, and their three kids were chased from their farm by the Russian army and had to flee by foot from Yugoslavia to Germany. With just a small hand cart full of their belongings, you can say that he truly started his life over with nothing but the clothes on his back and four (five, if you include his) mouths to feed. Despite this, when he retired, he had more money coming into his bank account each month than when he worked. He once even took an eight-week vacation to Spain. He drove a new car. How was this possible? Because—outside of his job— he had created Forever Cash that supported both him and my grandmother for as long as they lived. He used his job to provide temporary stability and used a little bit of his time (and, more importantly, his mind) to find ways to create that ongoing passive income. As a result of that, he had more money after retiring than he had when he was working.

You can do the same. I never got the chance to ask my grandfather more about his philosophy, his principles, and his methods. By the time I myself woke up from my long-lasting brain-fog about how to deal with money, my grandfather had unfortunately already passed away. I still, however, remember some of his words which, back then, didn't make any sense to me, but they do make sense to me now. Words like:

Don't say you are poor. Say you are broke, because being broke is temporary, but being poor is a mindset that will be permanent.
Look poor on paper, but have all the money in your back pocket.
Between $1 made and not spent, you have made $2.

While this last expression is not entirely mathematically correct, it illustrated for me the point that if you spend the money you make on useless stuff, you will have to work *twice* as hard to get ahead in life. It would be like having to make two dollars' worth of effort: one to get the balance back to zero (earning back the dollar you just wasted) and one to make another dollar that you can now save. Instead, the first step toward financial security is to simply stop throwing money away stupidly. Put that money to the side for future use in investments. If you do just that, you only worked once and still got ahead.

And he was also knowledgeable in taxes, which allowed him to "look poor on paper" and minimize his taxes, yet "have cash to spend in his pockets."

You might be reading this book because you are hoping to find a way out of a dead-end job or a way out of a stressful but high-paying career or to get away from a bad boss. I get it, and I want you to be able to quit your job. Just not yet!

If you were to quit today, you would have to *first* generate whatever your current total amount of monthly expenses is to just pay your regular bills and then on *top* of that you have to generate the extra additional cash needed to make the investments that will give you your Forever Cash. So by quitting your job *now* you basically put yourself in a hole and you will need to work *extra* hard to get out of that hole. You will have to spend a good part of the day just trying to make the money you need to live on and then the rest to make more money.

If that is how it would be for you, then I recommend that you do *not* quit your job *yet* but that you use it—as I said—as a launching pad. Although we all know there is no such thing as a truly safe and secure job because they can fire you any time, use your job as a somewhat reliable but temporary source for the money you need to at least pay the bills.

We all know that most jobs don't require your entire mental, physical, and emotional dedication. Look at how much time you spend at your job on Facebook, LinkedIn, YouTube, Google, or any other pages that have nothing to do with your job. Or, look at how often you take breaks and stand around the coffee pot or the break room, chit-chatting and gossiping with your colleagues. I know it happens; I have been there. In 2012, the average American today spends more than 700 minutes per month on Facebook. (To look up some interesting statistics on how much time we are wasting, go to www.ForeverCash.com/time.) That is more than twenty-three minutes a day, and it is increasing. Does

Facebook pay your bills? Does Facebook pay you a retirement check? That is almost twelve hours a month that you could use for education or research or making money outside of your job, in the evenings, and on the weekends. And, ideally, it should be ways that do *not* require you to trade hours for dollars as you do in your job, but ways that build up leverage over time. With leverage here, I don't mean financial leverage (like buying something with financing) but income leverage, meaning where you perhaps spend ten hours on a project but make $20,000 as a result of it.

Or maybe you send one e-mail to a list of e-mail subscribers you have built up and make $10,000 as a result of that. All of this is possible and will get you to your goal of quitting your job much more quickly, but it has nothing to do with trading dollars for hours as most people do in their jobs.

Once you are generating more cash on the side than you are in your job, then it is time to quit your job, because—at that point—your job becomes a liability. Imagine if you truly make as much money in one to two hours a day or in a few hours a weekend as you make in your job! Think about how much *more* you could make if you had the additional eight to nine hours a day that you currently spend *inside* an office working for *someone else*?

You get the point. Until that is the case, my recommendation is that you look at your job as an enabler of your financial future. If you hate your job it's even better; that discontent with your job will fuel you forward toward a better financial future. People who are comfortable where they are do not break out and do something new. It's the ones in pain who make the move. Use your job as a source of motivation to charge hard toward getting rid of it.

At the same time, think of it as something you are thankful for—even if it *is* going to be short-term—because it helps you finance and fund your quest toward financial freedom. It is paying your bills for you.

And I believe with this new way of looking at money with the tools that I will give you, you could be able to quit your job *forever* within three to five years and never have another one for the rest of your life.

You might want to challenge me on that and get it done faster. After all, once I got into action, it only took me ten months to get it done. If, after you got rid of your job, you continue on this path for just a few more years, you will be wealthy beyond what you currently can even imagine. I truly believe this; I have lived it.

I have applied what I call the Wealth Wheel process.

Chapter 9

THE WEALTH
WHEEL PROCESS

The previous chapters were an important part of hopefully getting you to see the world in a different light, and I hope some of the observations of how the poor and the wealthy handle and view their money have changed the way you looked at life.

By now, you know the importance of Forever Cash and Temporary Cash versus One-Time Cash.

You know that if you use your money not to get a new Harley-Davidson but instead to invest in something that provides Forever Cash, you will be able to buy many Harleys over the years and still keep that cash flow going.

That leaves one main question. How do I actually go about doing this?

This goes to the heart of the wealth mechanics! To generate the Forever Cash that we need to live the life we want to live, we need to apply the Wealth Wheel process.

Once you have the basics down, you will find it easy to increase your income *outside* of your job, decrease your expenses (or keep them low), and invest the money now saved into assets that bring you the cash flow that will set you free.

In summary, the Wealth Wheel process consists of:

- Making money (from your job and from extra income you will learn to create)
- Turning that money over into more and more money
- Investing that money into Forever Cash Assets
- Taking some of that cash flow and adding it to the money from your other income
- Taking both piles of money and then investing that larger pile of money into an additional asset for more cash flow
- Repeating that process again and again in ever larger amounts

While you are doing this process, you also pay off your debt and keep your expenses low—until you are out of the hamster wheel of financial hell.

So, yes, saving is part of this process. Saving for a few months to invest sounds like standard advice, and it probably is.

The difference here is that I am not telling you to save for forty years and only use the money when you are old, but instead to save only for as long as it takes to have enough money to turn the savings into a stream of Forever Cash. In other words, you don't save to spend, but to invest. Another differentiation is that you do not use the earnings from your investments for anything *but* further investments until you are done and have replaced your active income with Forever Cash. By doing that, you get to that next investment ever more quickly.

Another key to making the Wealth Wheel work is *not* letting the expenses increase as the income increases. One key here—at least for the first few years—is not to fall for anything that increases your overall expenses without adding more cash flow. This means no new car, no new house to live in (*yet*), and no super expensive trip to Vegas. Instead, just keep putting that money to the side and reinvesting it again and again in both Forever Cash and additional education that allows you to move faster and faster.

You should invest in whatever education, knowledge, and skills you need on how to make *more* money and how to generate more cash flow. That is absolutely necessary. As much as I want to think that you can take this book and run, chances are you will need some more detailed information on how to build and generate more money from home, without employees, without much overhead, and while you have a job. You can find a lot of education on the Internet. If you want to cut through the clutter, go to www.ForeverCash.com/education.

On the other hand I do understand that you need to celebrate your advancements, so I do also want you to reward yourself. I am therefore okay with you spending a little money to reward yourself *after* you hit certain milestones. For example, one milestone might be your first success making extra money. These rewards should not be abused and should not consist of more than 5 percent of what you made in an investment or in extra money per month. I, for example, love traveling as well as the newest electronic toys. Every time I complete either a particularly good real estate deal that makes me, let's say, $50,000 dollars, or when I hit any other major milestone like having reached a new goal in terms of monthly Forever Cash, I reward myself with a new Bose Mini stereo system or the newest Apple product (usually not more than a few hundred dollars). Or I book my family on a nice vacation in a five-star hotel to celebrate, recharge, and mainly just enjoy the feeling that I am actually enjoying the fruit of my labor. And while such a trip might cost a few thousand dollars for just a couple of days, it is an earned reward, that doesn't bring with it any ongoing monthly increase in spending. It's a one-time reward. After that I go back to my regular lifestyle and focus on increasing Forever Cash without increasing expenses. It's not yet time to get a new car, move to a bigger house, or get that vacation property you want. This, done too early, can be the end of the progress and the beginning of the end.

I have seen that this part is really the hardest part of my system, because at the core it talks about delayed gratification. You have probably heard about the Stanford marshmallow experiment from 1972. Conducted by psychologist Walter Mischel, the experiment gave preschoolers the choice of eating one marshmallow now or two in fifteen minutes. One third of the children were able to hold out the fifteen minutes and get their second marshmallow, while the rest couldn't take it. Forty years later, those who waited were found to have had a better quality of life and more success in life. They had fewer problems with drugs and obesity, were more in control of their lives overall, better able to plan ahead, deal with stress, and had more financial success.

That is not a coincidence.

Delayed gratification does not come naturally; it must be taught. We are trained to get instant gratification, and I am sorry to say it, but excessive instant gratification destroys your financial future, period. There is no other way to say that. The rich buy the luxuries in life last; the poor and average people buy them first. We are wired to spend money. Culturally, we have been trained to do that again and again and again. To succeed with the new way of living that I am recommending in this book, you have to rewire yourself in the way you think about money. But it's not easy.

This will be difficult, because when you follow this program, you will soon have saved thousands of dollars, and you will be investing this into something that might only equal $300 to $400 of Forever Cash income per month, which won't impress your friends and doesn't sound sexy. But that $300–$400 will be coming in forever, or close to it, meaning that with it you could pay your electric or heating bill for the rest of your life. Do it again and you will have your electric/heating bill and your car payment paid for life. Do it one more time and you have also your car insurance and your gas paid for life. And do it a few more times over the next few years, and soon you look around and see that all your expenses are paid for by Forever Cash.

That's where you need to have a plan. You need to plan for this. You need to make sure you can't easily spend the money you have set aside—not even for minor emergencies.

Spending the money you had earmarked for an investment on something else even happens to people who were well on their way to financial independence. Someone I have known forever told me a few years ago that they purchased two rental houses at incredibly low prices that provided huge monthly cash flow. When I heard that, I was excited because finally someone was getting the concepts I have been explaining to my friends for so long. However, just recently, she sold them because they had gone back up in value so much that she could make $50,000 in CASH profits from the sale. So she chose to convert the $50,000 value increase to cash in her pocket to pay off some bills and buy a new car. What she didn't realize was that she effectively sold the golden goose. She sold off a cash flow of more than $500 a month (and growing, as the mortgage was being paid down) a month for life in exchange for a new car that will be worthless a few years from now.

I know exactly how this happens—when you just spend what you make—because that was my life, too, until about 2002.

When I was in high school, I had my first part-time job in a liquor store, helping people carry cases of beer to their car. I made about $300 a month, and I managed to spend it. Then I went to serve in the German military and made about $400 a month. I had room and board for free, of course (and the food wasn't bad), and guess what? I managed to spend it all and had a $0 bank account at the end of the month. I went to college and— although college is free in Germany—I always had jobs part-time and made more than $1,000 and sometimes even as much as $2,000 a month. Guess what? My bank account at the end of every month? It was still zero. The same thing happened when I had a $50,000 job. Heck, I even had to sometimes borrow money to make it over to the next month because I spent it all. It's as if I had turned the water in my bathtub on but not put a plug in the drain, so the money was flowing out as fast as it was coming in.

Only when I understood how this process works, and how this process has been serving the rich and "old money" for centuries, and is the oldest form of getting wealthy, did I change my ways.

Because I now have truly internalized it and understood that each time we spend our hard earned money on worthless stuff, we move backward. Each time we invest it into something that brings us closer to Forever Cash, we are one step closer to true abundance and financial independence.

When you truly get it, you understand that it is here that you truly either win or lose in the financial game of life because these smaller monthly Forever Cash streams add up quickly.

Let's look at a scenario over just five years.

Year 1

You find a way (following the advice later in this book) to make an extra $1,000 a month net after taxes. That part is easy. That means you just generated an extra $12,000 a year.

After Year 1, you invest that into, let's say, a $60,000 rental property that you rent out for $850. You use the $12,000 as a down payment and therefore take a mortgage of $48,000 and realize a monthly cash flow of $350 on that property. Yes, such properties exist in many places around the United States. Not necessarily in New York City, or San Francisco, but you just have to start looking outside your geographic area. I personally own quite a few of them and have them managed by property management companies, so they are hands off for me.

Year 2

In Year 2, you now have taken your extra cash from $1,000 per month to $2,000 per month because you now have one year more of experience on how to make money on the side and have gotten better at it. In addition, you have the $350 per month Forever Cash Flow from your rental house.

That makes:

Total of $24,000 for the extra income: (12 × $2,000)

Approximately $4,200 cash flow from the first rental house: (12 × $350)

Total extra income: $28,200

With that, you now can buy two more rental properties at $60,000 each and put down $14,100 for each of them, meaning you only have $46,000 mortgages on each. Your payment is slightly lower than in the first property.

Now you are making $370 per month per property on each of the two new ones, and you are still making $350 a month on the first one.

Total Forever Cash income after two years: $1,090 (one time, $350; two times, $370 per month)

Year 3

The $1,090 per month adds up to $13,080 a year.

And if you just were able to increase your extra money income from $2,000 a month to $4,000 a month (after all you have had two years to learn and build up your ability to make money on the side) you now have an extra $48,000 from that too.

Total extra income: $61,080 a year

With that, you now can buy a ten-unit apartment complex that cash flows at $2,000 a month.

You are now up to $3,090 a month in Forever Cash income.

Year 4

Assuming the extra cash stays at $4,000 a month, this is another $48,000 a year.

The rental income is now around $37,080 a year.

Total income equals $85,080.

That will buy you another ten- to twelve-unit apartment complex, making you another $2,000 in Cash Flow forever each month, or a total of more than $5,090 a month, or $61,080 a year.

At this point, you have reached what most people need to retire from their jobs.

If you continue *one* more year, here is how the numbers play out.

Year 5

Extra income from your extra income source: another $48,000.

Income from rental real estate: $61,080.

Total extra income: $109,080

Buy with that a twenty-unit apartment complex or ten pieces of land that you can sell with seller financing and $300 a month payments for fifteen years that makes you $3,000 a month (= $36,000 a year).

At the end of year five you are up to $8,090 per month or $97,080 in just long-term Temporary Cash as well as Forever Cash per year, and you still have your $48,000 a year in extra income that you can choose to continue forever.

Most people are by now entirely financially free.

Year	Extra Cash Earned (Per Mo.)	Assets Acquired	Forever Cash Generated From Asset	Forever Cash Generated (Per Year)
1	$1,000	---	$350	$4,200
2	$2,000	1 Rental House	$1,090	$13,080
3	$4,000	3 Rental Houses	$3,090	$37,080
4	$4,000	8 Rental Houses	$5,090	$61,080
5	$4,000	8 Rental Houses & 10 Unit Apartment	$8,090	$97,080

And if you continue this for just a few more years, you can see how you can easily get over $200,000 per year in passive Forever Cash Flow (or very long-term temporary cash).

The best part is, that because this is real estate, and because you will run this as if it is a business (it actually *is*; it's just not one you have to be at every day and one where you don't have to be in an office), you get all the real estate and business tax benefits and will have few taxes on the $109,000 in income. Another positive is that mortgages are more than paid by your tenants.

Most people think in a linear fashion. They think, "If I create one Forever Cash Flow stream a year that brings me $500 a month, it will take me twenty years to get to $10,000 a month." That is faulty thinking. Because you reinvest each new stream of Forever Cash and add it to your short-term savings, it helps fuel and speeds up the next investment and compounds each other. When you realize how these initially smaller numbers compound and fuel each other and add up to a nice, big number after just four to five years, I believe you will start looking at any financial transaction of your life differently. You might just start asking yourself with every expense you are about to make: "Do

I *really* need this?" and "Does it take me closer to my goal or away from my goal?" Those answers will change your behavior.

Can you get here faster?

You definitely can. What if you could make $50,000 or $100,000 a year in extra money? You can, of course, turbocharge this process. You can get the same or bigger results in half the time, or three to four times the result in the same length of time. You can either make more extra money, reduce the expenses more, or find investments with higher cash flow returns. You can do one of these turbo boosters, or you can apply a combination of them. Just follow the process.

Remember when I told you about the seminar attendee—the teacher who loved teaching and felt she would have to leave her beloved job so she could make a living?

We determined that she should use the cash she was making from the three rental houses (three times $500 each per month = $1,500 a month, or $18,000 a year) and save that. Add to that about $10,000 she could save from her income as a teacher. Add to that another $50,000 she was anticipating that she could generate with just a few simple land flips, following my land-flipping methods. That makes a total of $78,000 a year ready for investments. That should be plenty of money to invest in cash-flow items—in her case, it was rental homes— generating another $1,000 a month, and that equals $12,000 *every* year in cash. At the end of year 2, she could buy three more rental houses. At the end of year 3, she could buy another three. At the end of year 4, she could buy another four houses. At the end of year 5, she might possibly have even five houses.

After five years, she would have a total of twenty houses. Each house would spit out $500 in cash or—all twenty—$10,000 in cash.

Of course, she could have also chosen a different vehicle of Forever Cash. For example, she might have opted to buy mortgage notes that return 20–30 percent per year for many years. Technically, I would consider that Temporary Cash, not Forever Cash.

She could have purchased a small business like a coin laundry that she could have learned to manage in only a few hours a day. Her choice, though, was real estate. She loves it, and so do I. She had already gotten the education needed to learn how to manage these properties or how to manage the manager of these properties, so that she would not be woken up at midnight by calls about broken toilets. Managing real estate is easy, but it is a skill that needs to be learned. It shouldn't take more than a few weeks to learn it, but it does have to be learned. But think about it. Would you rather spend a few hours a week managing your property manager than working forty hours a week in a job? I think the answer is obvious. And it doesn't take more than a few hours a month to manage a whole set of properties at a high standard. I have a number of rental houses and—thanks to the processes in place—I don't get tenant calls, and I don't go pick up rent. It's just not needed—not for me and not for you. If you would like to get your hands on a few of the Property Management Tools we have, please just go to www.ForeverCash.com/tools.

Think about the process of generating Forever Cash through a Wealth Wheel as a bathtub. Each new cash flow investment is an additional faucet you install on top and that starts spitting out cash to help fill the bathtub up with money. However, when you fight the urge

to spend the cash flowing in on stuff that doesn't bring you closer to your goal, it's like you are firmly putting the plug into the bottom of the tub—nothing gets out unless you let it.

Each time the money in the tub reaches a certain level, you invest in yet another faucet (another cash-dispensing asset) that now helps fill the tub back up even faster than before. When you do it again and again, the investments happen more quickly. With that, the cash flow gets faster and faster. Each time you add another cash flow stream, another faucet is added and more water (i.e., cash) flows into the tub.

The power of compound interest

What if you are already making great money but are wasting it on things that will not get you ahead in life? Would you now consider cutting some expenses and rearranging your life to get there faster? I bet you would.

Here's a test: would you rather have a large house, a second home in the mountains (or at the lake, or at the beach), and a beautiful boat now— even though it would mean living in a shack when you are old? Or would you rather live in a decent (but smaller) house now, rent a vacation place and/or a boat a couple of times a year when you need access to them, but then have the means to be able to live in the large home and buy your second home with all the toys you want a few years from now? Your answer to that question defines whether you will succeed in this process.

To master the temptation of spending that money, here is what you can do:

Open *two* separate savings bank accounts.

Call the first account your "Investment Account." Put 95 percent of your newly generated income and 95 percent of all the profits from your investments, be it One-Time Cash, Temporary Cash, or Forever Cash, into that account. Destroy the debit cards and checks the bank gives you for that account, so that you are not tempted to waste the money. Instead, just use wire transfers that still—in most U.S. banks—require you to go down to the bank to wire the money to the party you do business with and purchase an investment from. That way you won't touch the money, and you just make deposits until you have enough cash in that account to place your next investment.

Call the second account your "Fun Account." Put 5 percent of your newly generated income and even 5 percent of your Forever and Temporary Cash profits into a rewards/fun account. Regularly use that to enjoy some of the extravagant things you love but which will not add to your wealth. Stuff like going to Vegas, or buying a new stereo for the car, or a $400 pair of shoes (for the ladies). I do stuff like that on a regular basis (okay, not the shoes), but I recognize what I'm doing. I am aware that taking money I get from my rental houses and buying a new couch, or even just an iPad, will mean that I can't use that money to further my path to financial abundance. But I also know that these rewards keep me going and let me enjoy the journey.

Here are a few ways to generate cash flow that you don't work for:

- Buy a rental house that is *cash flow positive* in an area of the United States where they are cheap. (Yes, there are areas of the United States where you can buy good houses for $50,000–$100,000 and rent them for $700 to $1,100.)

- Buy tax-lien certificates (Temporary Cash) that are secured by the government.
- Buy land and flip it with seller financing at a high interest rate (and high profit margins) (Temporary Cash).
- Buy dividend-paying stocks that pay annually (Forever Cash).
- Buy a mobile home lot with a mobile home on it and sell the home with seller-financing (Temporary Cash) but leasing the lot underneath (Forever Cash).
- Write and publish short books on Amazon.com for passive cash flow based on royalties (Temporary Cash).
- Apply stock options strategies for cash flow (Temporary Cash).
- Build online subscription services that people pay you monthly to be part of (Temporary Cash).
- Put up an Internet banner ad for an affiliate product and get commission when that product sells (technically One-Time Cash, but a good banner ad can produce many sales a day for a long time without having to change it and mess with it so it qualifies as Temporary Cash).
- Build a network marketing organization that is self-sustainable and provides monthly stable cash flow (Forever Cash, if built right).
- If you have more money to invest and you have some business experience, consider buying a simple cash-flow business that doesn't require a lot of time to manage (like a coin laundry or a small car wash; they are cash cows if done right) (Forever Cash).

Let's review how the money out there finds its way into your pocket.

- It's just the part of your job income that you managed to set aside that helps to fill the tub a few drops at a time.
- You create extra income outside of your job and use that, along with any other savings; you were able to build to buy your first Forever Cash Asset.

- It is one stream of cash from one asset that flows, plus the drops from your savings and your extra income.
- It is two streams of cash from two assets that flow, plus your savings and the extra income.
- Apply just a few of these and you have three, then four, then five streams of cash from your assets. Each adds more cash flow.
- Soon you have more cash coming in than you need to live on.

While you do that, you pay attention to not increasing your lifestyle and spending the cash.

Only when the tub is being filled fast enough by multiple streams of Temporary or Forever Cash income do you quit your job and allow yourself to increase your cost of living.

If you do fall for the urge to spend the money on worthless stuff, you are screwing things up. It will be just like you've pulled the plug out of the tub. I am sure you are now familiar with how that works and have done that a few times. So have I. You can't put in new money fast enough to make up for what goes down the drain when you spend it crazily.

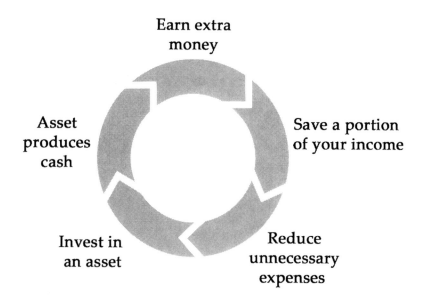

Once you have established one cash-producing asset, the picture changes a little.

As I said before, when I first got clear on this process, I can safely say that my drain plug was more or less nonexistent. I was working hard at my job, but the money was flowing *out* of the bottom of the tub. I was spending my hard-earned money on all sorts of things. I had a lot of bad debt (not the *good* kind, the kind we will talk about later on). I had student debt; I also had consumer loans for the furniture in my house, things like my couch, my bed, even for my refrigerator. Because I didn't wait to have these things but got them before I could afford them. I ended up becoming a source of Temporary Cash Flow to the financers. I even had a somewhat embarrassing consumer loan on a water softener I was stupid enough to buy from a door-to-door salesman.

Once I started to determine how I was mismanaging my money, and I decided which vehicle I wanted to use to create a Wealth Wheel (real estate, and then online marketing, for me), within ten months, all those loans were gone, and the cash flow was happening.

Although the cash flow at that time was not yet Forever Cash, we used that Temporary Cash to later establish a true Wealth Wheel. In our case, this cash and the Temporary Cash Flow was generated from selling land with seller financing; the buyers would pay us a down-payment and then made monthly payments. Often, the down-payment alone—plus a few monthly payments—was enough to pay for what we had invested initially to obtain the property, and then the monthly payments were passive cash flow and 100 percent profit. I like that kind of deal, but as I had said before, the only issue is that the payments will eventually stop someday once the land has been paid off. The fun will be over unless I keep buying and flipping more land. So real-estate *flipping* meant great cash and great cash flow, but not yet Forever Cash.

To establish a Forever Cash generating machine, we took (and keep taking) some of the money that we make from all our ways of earning income, including our land payments and cash sale payments, and from other investments, businesses and even from the more recent successes in network marketing and online marketing businesses and use that money to buy other kinds of cash flowing assets that provide permanent Forever Cash Flow for an indefinite period of time. We like assets like rental houses, multi-family apartment complexes, land that can be leased and even small businesses like coin laundries, car washes, and self-storage units, as well as some dividend stock. They are part of what we focus on. All of it is part of what keeps the cash flow growing and turns One-Time Cash and Temporary Cash into Forever Cash Flow, using the Wealth Wheel strategy.

If you don't take some off the table and invest it into something that secures you forever, you might find yourself some day in the same position as these people who come up to my live seminar saying, "Jack, I had it all, and I lost it all." You don't have to lose it all. Remember, even the largest money mountains can disappear, but a portfolio of Forever Cash Flow streams rarely, if ever, all disappear. One rental home might burn down but not all twenty. One banner ad might stop bringing in money but not all twenty you have around the web. One Amazon special report might stop selling but not all twenty-five books you have published. Multiple streams of Temporary and Forever Cash bring stability and freedom. Money mountains bring worries.

Chapter 10

BUSINESS IS NOT FOR EVERYONE, BUT CASH FLOW FREEDOM IS

First of all, let me tell you that I *love* businesses. I own and run a number of them; they are the number-one vehicle in the world to create wealth. Private enterprise is what creates wealth, brings up entire countries from poverty to wealth, and creates jobs that the masses can live on.

Starting, buying, or growing a business is probably the fastest way to make the money you need to, and to turn that income into a lot of passive ongoing Cash Flow Freedom. But before we go into detail about setting up a Wealth Wheel to make more money, I would like to clarify three things:

Starting, owning, and running a full-blown business is not for everyone. When I say this, I don't mean to say that I don't think you are capable of running your own business or that I don't recommend using a business to establish cash flow—on the contrary. If you are capable of running a real business, one with employees, office, perhaps a storefront—go ahead and do it.

Running a full-blown business with overhead, employees and even perhaps a brick-and-mortar location requires the business owner to be prepared. It takes a great deal of effort to bring up and run a successful business with all the bells and whistles. While it has the potential to be a great source of wealth and profits, some of which might even come in forever, not everyone is cut out to run a business and to handle the stress of not knowing where their next paycheck will be coming from. Not everyone is cut out to handle the extra work and time that comes with running their own business at the beginning. A start-up business typically requires the owner to do what an entire office staff would do, including being the receptionist, the materials purchaser, quality inspector, salesperson, human resources director, accounting department, and executive board. Chances are you are not equally good at all of these duties. You might get away with only doing one area well, but that won't allow you to grow as you need to do if you want to experience freedom and, as a result, your dream of starting your own company over time turns into a glorified job where you end up working more than before for the same or less money.

That is the sad truth. It comes back to the same issue I mentioned before. People don't spend time thinking about what it means to start a full-blown business and just see the results that some people (who had or developed the right skills) got with it. They don't see the 99 percent; they only see the 1 percent. Yet, according to the website Payscale.com, the median income for small business owners is only $67,000. Hardly worth it if you consider that it typically included both husband and wife working twelve-to-sixteen-hour days six to seven days a week. Yet, as you look around, there are many people advising you to start your own full-blown business, quit your job, and put your life savings on the line. While that is the right approach for *some*, I think for most it is not. More often than not, someone who starts a full business often needs to develop a whole new skillset first—a business skill set. Some people need to first work on other areas of their lives, areas without which they won't ever be successful in any business. They need to develop concrete skills in marketing, sales, management, math, accounting, as well as those less-tangible skills like self-confidence, leadership, emotional intelligence, and motivation. Because of this, I don't recommend that just *any*one go out, quit their job, and try to start a brick-and-mortar business. Although the idea is romantic, the reality is often a cold shower.

Before investing any money in starting or running a business, take a moment to evaluate your strengths and weaknesses as an entrepreneur. Instead of purchasing an air-conditioning repair company without knowing anything about the market or running of a small business, it may be better to start smaller. Instead, start developing the skills you need without risking thousands of dollars. Then, once you have built up your confidence and expertise, you can tackle the bigger money-making ideas.

Unfortunately, a lot of businesses fail due to poor planning, overconfidence of many entrepreneurs, and—most of all—their lack of business and financial management skills.

In my opinion, way too many people have started, bought, or taken over businesses without having a clue as to what it takes to run a business successfully. Too many people have put their pile of money that they have built up into a business only to have it wiped out financially after the business failed. That is not what we are talking about here. Therefore, I believe there is another way. There is a way that is less risky and yet more reliable in getting you where you want! The answer is to make money outside of your job in the form of a micro business, a venture that you treat as a business from a tax point of view. With a micro business, you can take advantage of all the tax benefits and loopholes for business owners, yet you do not need to have an office, overhead, storefront, or employees, and, most importantly, you do not need a lot of money to get started with. The focus of the kind of activity I suggest you do is to make extra money, not build a business structure and formal organization. You have most of the benefits without most of the problems of running a business.

Going down that path, you will learn to make more money, money which you then need to use as your seed money for your Wealth Wheel investing process. It's safe, predictable and doesn't require a large amount of business management skills. So, the solution is to create cash from home, and then use *that* cash to create Forever Cash Flow without having to have a full-blown business and lots of overhead.

Technically, because it is a business, you get to use all the tax benefits the "real" businesses get to use. That means you win twice—by running a lean operation from home that avoids the pitfalls the larger businesses have and by saving tons in taxes.

By avoiding high risk early in the game, you will be able to accomplish great things:

- Without putting your life savings on the line
- Without having to quit your job
- Without having to rent an office location
- Without having to hire any employees
- Without having to have a retail location

You need to learn how to use the best the system has to offer and reject that which doesn't serve you.

In today's virtual, highly connected, computer-based world, there is no reason for you to spend your life savings on something that has only a slim chance to succeed.

I will recommend that you start your own money-making venture/ project, and that you run this new money-making venture/project in the form of a business structure so you get all the tax benefits that were designed for businesses, but it will not necessarily be the type of business that you may have imagined so far. It might just be a part-time activity you use to sell stuff online, to flip a piece of real estate for profit, to write a book and publish it online, to play with some stock market option strategies, or to build a network marketing team around you. Many of my suggestions won't even feel like a business because you can do them by literally just applying a few hundred dollars to a project to get it started. It has low start-up costs and can even be done from your home computer, so it is nonthreatening. And that is important. You might be frustrated where you are in life right now, but you probably are not ready to put all your life savings on one card, quit your job, and just go for it. If you are like so many people I have met and talked to over the years, you are afraid of doing that step. I was, too, when I started. For many people starting out, this level of business is the right one, right now. Not only does it allow you to get started for cheap with high upside potential, it also allows you to learn valuable skills.

When my wife and I came to the conclusion that we needed to make extra money outside of our jobs, we realized we didn't have the first clue about things like marketing or selling, so we made a conscious choice to join a network marketing company. We did that at that time for two reasons: to make a ton of money (and we have since made a good chunk of money in network marketing) and to learn marketing in particular. We picked a great company that offered a great amount of training for new and existing members. For two years, we diligently attended meetings, learned the basic principles of marketing, and learned how to make a presentation (something I never had to do in my life). Since I lacked most of the basic entrepreneurial skills, the lessons I gathered from the training are helping me to this day. I credit a lot of my success later on to this. It helped me to start thinking like an entrepreneur, but without having to worry about the fulfillment behind it because that was taken care of by the company. I suggest you do the same thing. Be careful which organization you join, however. Some companies are stable, have been around for a long time, and will stay around for a long time, while others are fly-by-night companies. I have reviewed a lot of them and put together a list of the ones I consider to be okay at www. ForeverCash.com/mlm.

The same happened with a lot of the other things I did during this period, what I call now my "ramp-up period." I started educating myself on Internet marketing and real estate investing—while trying to figure out which of these areas would be the best fit for me.

All this allowed me to learn while making money, to avoid unnecessary expenses, and to build my cash and my cash flow faster. By the time I had built a nice amount of cash and Temporary Cash Flow, my skills had increased to the point that now I could take it to the next level and invest in Forever Cash Assets. I now knew how to manage them easily in minimal time (or how to manage the managers of the Forever Cash Assets). Once this process starts, it's like a whole new world opens up. You realize you are not forever doomed to live off the one income from your full-time job. Now the fun starts: Plan how you will invest your seed money to start generating passive income and enjoying Cash Flow Freedom.

I hope that—so far—you agree that you might see a slight glimpse of light at the end of the tunnel if what I am telling you is right.

Indeed, you can:

- Make some extra money outside your job in ways that don't take you away from your family for hours at a time
- Have the ability to live debt free (of bad debt, that is)
- Invest that money that can make you 10–30 percent ROI per year (and higher)

You are not destined to live off just your job income for the rest of your working days!

I said in the beginning that a business is not for everyone—but Cash Flow Freedom is. I hope I have demonstrated that you don't need to buy a Subway or a McDonald's franchise and manage dozens of employees to get cash flow forever. There are all kinds of ways for you to start generating more income today, now that you are seeing life through a new pair of financial "glasses." There are lots of different kinds of vehicles you can choose from when deciding how to invest your money and how to spend time building your Wealth Wheel. The vehicle that has worked well for me has been real estate, as well as Internet marketing (something I will explain further in the next chapters). Other vehicles are as mentioned—stock market investing, options trading, becoming an expert in something and teaching others how to do what you know. You'd be surprised and amazed what people consider to be an expertise and are willing to pay for. Topics like setting up home entertainment systems, websites (there are tons of people who make a great living teaching people how to put up and manage WordPress websites, something anyone can learn in a few days); organizing your office; doing social marketing—the list goes on and on. Even if you are not comfortable starting a new business, you don't have to. There are tons of other opportunities out there that will let you keep your job and use the money you make to invest in hands-off asset classes that provide cash flow—like, for example, dividend stock or investments in real estate investment trusts that pay high dividends. If you choose your asset well, over a short time it can and will eventually *replace* what you are earning in your job. And even here, make sure that for as long as possible you reinvest every penny you make from your investments into more investments so that the Wealth Wheel moves faster and faster.

As a result: Even if you *love, love, love* your job, or you just would never even dream of starting your own business, you can still go down the path toward creating Forever Cash Flow. Cash flow truly has something for everyone, no matter where you are in life. You don't have to run a complex business or even any business at all to create it.

Chapter 11

WHAT YOU CAN DO TO CREATE SEED MONEY

B y now, you probably have one burning concern: "Okay, Jack, while I understand how both the Wealth Wheel and the Forever Cash concepts work, I have no clue about where to start and how I can make extra money."

It's simple. The first step to getting started is to find ways to create *seed money*. The more sources you can find for seed money, the better. What is seed money? Seed money is money available to you for investments.

The easiest and fastest way to create seed money is to stop the leaks in your financial ship. Small leaks can, over time, sink even the best and the most powerful ship. Those leaks, of course, are all those unnecessary expenses that don't make a dent in your lifestyle when you remove them. Releasing them and putting them into your seed money/ investment account is a small but powerful tool to begin your financial advancement.

The sealing of those leaks will not necessarily add all that is needed to your seed money, but it is important on two levels. You want to increase your chances of success dramatically. Level one is in creating a habit of not letting expenses rise with income. The second (and more exciting) way to create seed money has to do with the way you use your time outside of your job.

I've heard it said that "From 8 a.m. to 5 p.m. you make a living; from 5 p.m. to 10 p.m. and on the weekends, you make a fortune." Except for the few people who have made their fortune by rising through the ranks from lower-level employees to get to the top, this has been true. For every ten who have made their fortune in corporate America, there are probably 1,000 who have not and got stuck somewhere in the middle without freedom and the only thing they get to take home is extra work for the weekend and late nights at the computer. If you are already working hard, why not work hard on something that brings *you* forward instead of just the company you work for?

"But, Jack," you may say. "I don't have any time outside of my job. I work hard all week, and I need to relax when I get home." I understand how you feel; I felt the same way when I was working full-time for a large company. Remember: We all have the same twenty-four hours per day to use the best we can. The average person sleeps about seven to eight hours per night, plus about ten for working and commuting, so that leaves us with six hours per day, or about thirty per week (from Monday to Friday) and leaving the weekends for rest and for spending time with the family. Imagine what would happen if we took just ten of those thirty hours to invest in our future. I am always amazed by how many friends who have jobs answer my Facebook posts while they are at their jobs. It does seem a great many people have some time—while on the job—to do other things. Perhaps you have one of those jobs where you can sneak in an hour of Forever Cash education or research a few times a week.

Another aspect I also get is that not everyone is starting at the same spot. While some people with high-paying jobs or with already successful companies will be able to use money from their daytime activities to invest in a cash flow that generates assets by simply deviating some of their income to that, or by cutting down their lifestyle from luxury to just plain comfort for a while, others don't have that option. Most people, actually, will have to find some other sort of way of making some money over and beyond their income from their job and try their hardest not to spend that extra income. What are some options?

I'd like to go into a little more detail about some practical ways you can make extra money outside of your full-time job. By no means are these the only ones out there. There are a million different ways you can make extra money. And remember, I am not talking about permanently working yourself ragged to achieve financial security. Instead, I'm talking about working smarter and harder now for a limited time, long enough to get the Wealth Wheel going and to a decent level, but not so much that you don't have time for anything else (unless you just want to, of course). After you get the Wealth Wheel going and have placed your first few Temporary Cash and/or Forever Cash investments, the cash or cash flow from the first few assets will pay for the next ones, and those will pay for the next ones, and so on in an ever-faster fashion.

It all starts with seed money.

Don't limit yourself to what others around you are doing. Think outside the box and locate some new opportunities that others may have passed over. Look at the people (outside of your family and coworkers) and try to see what kind of need they have. Is there a hole in their daily lives that you can help to fill? Think practically, and use your imagination. Remember, this chapter is not a complete list of suggestions: it is a guideline to get you to think along the right lines.

Option 1: Be a problem solver

As you examine ways to make your seed money, begin to think outside the box. There are traditional ways of making money—like working longer hours or getting a part-time job—that may help you to get to your goal, but that will diminish the quality of your life in the meantime. Go for it, I say, if—after reading this entire book—you see that this is the only way available to you to make more money. What I am more interested in is getting you into a new frame of thinking. You must get into a frame of mind where you don't necessarily have to exchange lots of hours for money. If you limit yourself to trading time for money, you will never reach your full earning potential.

Think about it: If someone like Bill Gates had to rely on hourly wages, he would never be able to make as much as he does even if he worked twenty-four hours a day, every day! Hourly is not the way to go, or only as a last resort.

A key to finding new ways of making money is to learn to identify opportunities and, most importantly, solve problems.

There is a saying: Luck is found at the intersection of Opportunity and Preparation. I do believe that somewhat, but I like to take it a step further. I don't believe in luck. I don't believe in sitting back and waiting for things to happen to you. I believe in *making* your own luck happen. I believe in looking for opportunities and being prepared to act when you see them. It's just funny how many people have told me how lucky I am that I have such a great life. Really? It wasn't luck at all. Instead, I spent countless hours studying all kinds of business options and opportunities until I found what worked for me. Then, I took action and made it happen. If *that* is luck, then I *am* lucky.

How can you find these opportunities?

I believe that Opportunity is found at the intersection of Problems and Attention.

I believe you make your own luck when you become aware of your surroundings, when you pay attention to what is happening in the world around you, and when you hear what people are complaining about and what problems they are experiencing. When you start being aware of all of that *and* you have the right preparation (like an education on how to fix their problems), then you are presented with an opportunity. In other words, any identified problem and any problem that is generating attention means you have the seed of opportunity.

Every product and *every* item you have ever seen, bought, or used solves a problem. If you buy a hammer, it's because you had a problem of getting a nail into a wall, and you lacked the tool to do it. Cars were invented because horses tired too quickly and were too slow—not to mention that, even in the stall when they were not at work, horses were costing the owner money. A better solution had to be found, and the car was invented.

When the phone was invented, it was to solve the problems of long distance communication. When the sidewalk was invented, it was to solve the problem of pedestrian deaths by being run over by horses or cars. When you buy a lollipop, it's to solve the problem of craving something sweet. When you buy a movie ticket to watch a funny movie, it's to solve the problem of being bored or wanting to escape reality for two hours and delve into a fantasy world.

Everything you see in the real world is a solution to a problem. Billions are being made every day by people who solve problems. Finding the right tool for *you* to make more money means that you will have to focus on what problems exist in the world and then solve just one or two of them. All it takes is to solve one problem well, and you might be set for life.

Problems are all around you. Just listen to people when they talk to you. We all love to talk about what's not working, what we don't like, and what we wish would be different. That is what you want to look out for. Listens for phrases like: "I wish ... would be different;" "I can't stand that ..." or "I hate how ...." You don't have to invent the better mousetrap or invent something that solves the problems of this world. Just listen to your every conversation with people; you will hear lots of problems. As you get used to listening to the problems, the solutions will pop out to you. It's like magic. One moment they are invisible; the next moment, you see these solutions and opportunities everywhere.

Let me share with you one of my first successes in identifying opportunity and seizing it. In the year 2000, when I was still just a little cog working for a big corporate machine, the Compaq iPAQ, one of the first true handheld devices came out. It had Pocket Word, Pocket Excel, Pocket Internet Explorer, Tasks, Contacts, Notes, and Voice Recorder. It was the coolest thing ever back then. In the era before smartphones and iPads, the idea of combining a personal agenda, phone calls, and (I think) Internet access, all controlled with a stylus, was revolutionary. They were flying off the shelves.

One day, while speaking with my colleagues, they mentioned how they had seen on television that these things were selling at a retail price of $450 but how, because of the high demand and limited supply, they were being bought online (through eBay) for $650. One of my coworkers even mentioned how he had seen a few at a local store the night before.

In the weeks and years before that, I would have just shaken my head and laughed about the craziness of people going out of their way to buy tools like these on eBay for more than they sold retail in the store, but this time something different happened. The thought came up that perhaps this was an opportunity to make some money.

I identified the issues—the pros and the cons. They were: 1) Not enough of these handheld devices were being produced; and 2) There seemed to be a distribution problem because they were sold out in many stores; 3) I happened to be located near one of the stores that still had some; and 4) I identified the solution: Buy some at the local store and sell them online on eBay the next day.

That night, I went to the store and bought two of these handheld devices for $450 each using my credit card. (I had no cash and was still paying off my student loans and car). Without opening the packages, I immediately listed them online on eBay. Within three days, both auctions had closed, and both sold for $650, just like predicted. The winning bidders sent me the money (and also paid for shipping), and I promptly sent the devices to them. Then I sat back and enjoyed the fact that I had just made $400 cash profit for simply solving someone else's problem.

Deals like that are out there all the time. Do you remember Tickle Me Elmo and how much they were in demand a few Christmas seasons ago? Or how certain cell phones sell for a considerably higher price on eBay when they are mostly sold out in the stores?

Education is your preparation to solve problems, and I don't mean a college education. When you are prepared to actually use the business knowledge and investment tools you have acquired, you might be able to take an opportunity you see and to act on it. I can promise you that, if you don't even have an awareness of what's going on around you, and if you are not aware of possible solutions, you won't ever realize an opportunity.

Once you get used to listening out for problems, all you need to do is think, "How can this be solved?" and then look for a solution. If you can find a reasonable solution to the problem, it will sell. If you just apply this thinking for a few weeks, you will start seeing opportunity at every corner. After that, it will only be a matter of learning the tools you need to take advantage of these opportunities. You will be well on your way.

I have made a lot of money since those eBay sales, but that first $400 I will never forget. It showed me that I don't have to trade hours for dollars in my job, and it gave me hope that there is a way out of this that can give me financial security and freedom outside a job forever. And almost to the day, four years later I was able to quit my job. No, it didn't happen overnight, but it happened faster than I could ever have thought.

Option 2: Be a contrarian and use cycles

In business, many things happen in cycles. Real estate certainly does, but so does the stock market. In certain months of the year, the stock market is notoriously bad; in other months, it is traditionally good. Everything has its time, and the psychology of the masses define that.

When everyone is excited for real estate, prices jump like crazy. When everyone is excited about stocks, prices will jump like crazy. When everyone is running from real estate or stocks, prices fall.

I find it difficult to time the market, but I find it easy to go against an existing trend. Simply put:

When the market crashes, *buy*.

When the market soars, *sell*.

This knowledge applies to real estate as much as to stocks and to any other investment that operates cyclically.

For example: Let's examine the big bank stock during the bank bailout crisis. When the big banks were about to fail, everyone sold stock at a loss. That would have been the time to load up on bank stock; a few months later, they were back to three to five times as high.

For example: Let's take Wells Fargo Bank. In the middle of the crisis, its stock dropped from the $30 range down to the $8 range, only to go back up in the $25 range a short two months later. Want to make some extra money? Buy large, crucial company stock when it is in a crisis. It is my experience that they either find a way to fix it, and the stock recovers, or if they are truly "too big to fail," the federal government steps in to help them. I don't condone government bailouts, but we can't change it, either … so, why not use events like this to make some money? Your stock has a high chance of making some killer returns if you have the guts to do the opposite of what the masses do and act contrarian.

At the same time, you might want to get out of the stock market if the market is soaring or, at least, use some of your earnings to buy insurance—like some put options—that allow you to sell your stock at a certain price for a certain time. While you have to pay for these options, they do guarantee that you make some profits. You effectively lock down your profits for a certain time period. Remember, though, that it is impossible to time the market. Once it goes down, it often goes down fast, so one week or longer of a holding time can destroy much of your profits. It might be better to take some of the money you made off the table a bit earlier.

Here is another example. When the real estate market broke down, and prices in some areas went down by 70 percent in many areas, what did most people do? They shied away and swore to never get involved in real estate again. Yet, it wasn't real estate that failed them. It was their inability and lack of education to see that things weren't sustainable. As a result, nobody was touching houses, and the Phoenix, Arizona, real estate market had 50,000 houses on the market. *That* would have been the time to buy houses. Yet, every article in the local newspapers warned, "Stay away from houses. Prices might go further down." While that was possible, of course, I started buying houses in March 2009 when the market hit an all-time low. Nobody wanted to buy, but—to the contrarian smart investor—the key was not whether prices were at an all-time low; the key was that the numbers for buying these houses as investment rental homes now made a lot of sense. At these extremely low prices (some houses sold for $20 to $40 per square foot, meaning a 1,000 square foot, three- bedroom, two-bath house sold often for under $40,000), these properties produce attractive Forever Cash Flows even if you finance them to 100 percent. A true contrarian opportunity seeker would have ignored what the media was saying at that time and just analyzed the opportunity by looking at the numbers. And the numbers made amazing sense.

Because I consider myself a hard-core contrarian, this is what I did and I went and bought a batch of fifteen rental houses. It didn't matter to me what the media said about the potential of the market going down another 40 percent— as some media outlets were reporting—because I bought these houses for their potential to bring in Forever Cash. With Forever Cash, my preferred holding time is just that … Forever. I saw no reason to wait any longer. The newspaper articles were correct in that they were lamenting a reduction of value of more than 70 percent from the peak of the market. But that was just a bad thing if you either owned a house that you bought before the collapse of the real estate market, and now you saw their value go down and further down every year. As a cash flow investor with a holding period of forever, all I needed to look for was the answer to the question: "If I buy this property now, will I be satisfied with the cash flow the property throws off?" My answer to that was a clear and resounding, "Yes!"

I took the plunge and bought some, then some more, and them some more. The first one I totally over improved and spent a lot more on repairs than I should have. But at the prices I bought them, I still made great money every month and continue to do so. Then I learned from these mistakes and over time made less and less. Those properties produce about $500 per house in positive cash flow every single month and, on top of it, in the following three years, they have gone up in value by over 60 percent—on average. I love the Forever Cash Flow, and I hope you get that it doesn't matter if they go up or down in value. I have no intention of selling them any time soon. I would only consider selling them if I had another investment that I could roll them over and into that gives me a higher cash-on-cash return than these houses do. In the meantime, I have had cash of more than $10,000 a month come in from these houses while I owned them and made an extra $700,000 in equity appreciation when I sell them.

The key here is to invest when everyone is scared. Although that sounds like a scary concept in itself, it is not. As a true Forever Cash investor, you don't care what the people say; you listen to what the numbers say. And if the numbers scream "deal, deal, deal," you act. Remember the neighbors, friends, and newspapers don't pay your bills. Only you do. Listen to the numbers, and you will be fine.

I take my contrarianism to another level. I apply it to almost everything. I invest in land because most other real estate investors go after houses. Therefore, they leave the huge area of land investments all up to me and a few of my students.

I also apply this in my personal life. When I hear that an earthquake struck Mexico, I want to buy a ticket to Mexico. While that sounds irresponsible, I would like for you to check out how the media really reports on an event. And it's all about hype. If a storm hits a city and topples three trees and two cars on one street, the media is not going to show the 99.9 percent of the city that was left unharmed. No, they will focus on that one street that is in disarray. That is how they get viewers.

Nobody tunes in to see a perfectly fine city. That wouldn't be news. But a few toppled trees and turned over cars? Now that is something that catches people's attention. It is like that for almost all media reports. Most media reports are over exaggerated, but the masses still believe them. As a result, prices for flights to such locations and hotels in such places are cheap during these times.

If everyone runs in one direction and creates huge competition in that direction, look the other way and search for opportunities there. They will be easier to find, with less competitors and higher profit margins.

Option 3: Do part-time work outside your current job

Just like the day I made the $400 for these Compaq iPAQs handheld devices in a few days *outside* of my job, there are many ways to make money *outside* of your job, or even *inside* your job, or even with an *additional* job.

One way to find an additional income source outside of your job is to think of your passions in addition to what you are good at as well as your surroundings and how you could earn money from them.

Make a list of all the stuff you are good at. This list can be as simple or mundane as you want it to be.

Think about what people compliment you on, your style of clothing (people need a fashion advisor). Perhaps you keep your household organized. Perhaps you are skilled in something. Perhaps you can take complex matters and break them down into simple steps. In terms of being passionate, think about all the things you love but perhaps haven't spent much time doing or studying up on.

It could be anything. How about LEGOs? As a kid, you probably liked to play with those plastic LEGO cubes and build towers with them. I know I did. It's not just for boys, either. My daughter *loves* her LEGOs. Did you know that there is a great amount of LEGO collectors out there who pay top dollar for discontinued sets of LEGOs? As a matter of fact, I met a man at a conference I attend who spends a little time each week buying and selling sets of LEGOs. Over a few glasses of wine, I learned that whenever LEGO comes out with a new set, the company usually only produces that one set for anywhere from twelve to eighteen months. Then, that set is discontinued, and the next sets come out. This man goes and buys some of the most popular sets (like the Star Wars sets, for example) and buys multiples of them (toward the end of their production time). He keeps them in his house in storage for anywhere between a few weeks to a few months. After that time or any time he needs the money, he lists a few of the ones that are now out of production on eBay and sells them often for two to five times (or more) what he bought that set for. One sale sometimes makes him several hundred or even several thousand dollars in profits.

Overall, he has about $60,000 in inventory right now that he could—today—sell for more than $200,000 in profits.

You thought LEGO was just for children? Think again, there are some serious profits in these kinds of collectors' items. You just have to know they exist and what to look for.

How about something totally different? Perhaps you live in an area that is rich with history, but you have noted that there is no one taking advantage of it. Why not offer your services as a tour guide? You could set up a website, get yourself registered, and offer walking tours or vehicle tours of certain parts of your town with historic meaning. While being a tour guide is technically exchanging time for money, at least there is one scalable factor here. You don't just have to do one-on-one tours, but you can do group tours so you make more money in the same time guiding more people around to historic locations.

Perhaps you are handy with computers or with surround sound and TV set-ups. For example, I can't even figure out how to connect the cable box to the TV, let alone make the DVR, DVD, and the surround sound system all work together. When we moved into our house, I literally had just the TV connected to the cable box (which the cable guy connected) in one room and that was the only TV running. Anyone wanted to watch TV somewhere else? Sorry, not working! Anyone who wanted to watch a DVD, sorry! It wasn't possible, because it was not connected. While we don't watch much TV at all at home—there is nothing that brings you forward in life watching TV, anyway—so it wasn't a big deal, but it's still nice to have it all set up. I called a company to finish the installation. They charged me $150 per hour and sold me another $2,000 in equipment so I could control all my TV and video equipment from one remote—from anywhere in the house and even from my iPhone. I am only providing this example to show that certain knowledge— like the knowledge of how to set these things up— has value and, in some cases, a *lot* of value. There are people like me who would rather eat my shoe than set up a home entertainment system. I would rather pay someone $150 per hour to get it done. If you know how to set up home entertainment systems, offer that skill on Craigslist for $50 per hour, and you will get some jobs. Five hours of this a week equals twenty hours a month equals $1,000 a month, or $12,000 a year. Along with a few savings, you can start your Wealth Wheel process, and you will get things started well.

How about this? Do you know a little about how the stock market works? Do you know how to trade options? Do you know "put options," "call options," "straddles," and other terms like that? Are you willing to learn? Are you aware there are strategies where you can sell one kind of option that has a low likelihood of ever being exercised, meaning you get paid for selling these options and most likely get to keep that money? If you are uncomfortable with that, you can spend some of the money you just receive on the opposite kind of option, protecting your position for the case that the first option does get into the money, and the buyer does exercise it. If you know how to do that —in a conservative way with the right options in the right circumstances—you can create fairly reliable cash flow month after month after month from such option deals. While not a passive cash flow asset in themselves, they can be a good way to make some money on the side to put into your Wealth Wheel process.

Does this sound exciting? Or did it just sound like Chinese? If it sounded like Chinese, don't get frustrated; see it as a sign that you need to learn, because those who understand these transactions make a lot of money while others work in jobs. I met a man from Germany one time at a seminar who had taken this to heart. While having a job in

Germany, he figured out how to make an options cash flow. He now travels the world with his wife, making over $100,000 a year. All he needs to maintain that income is Internet access, so he can continue making his option deals. While his current focus is not on Forever Cash, he still has figured out how to make over $100,000 per year in extra money—part-time.

Last, if you see nothing else working and are looking for a way to make a few extra bucks, consider getting a part-time job for a few months. Working just ten to fifteen hours a week extra even at a low hourly rate can easily generate (at least) $150–$300 per week or $600–$1000 per month (which comes to $7,200–$12,000 a year), even if you do something fairly basic. Even if you still need to pay taxes on that money, chances are that you won't pay much in taxes. Be honest for a minute: Would you feel embarrassed by taking a part-time job in addition to what you already do? You might feel that way, and it would be understandable. Remember what I said earlier: Your neighbors and coworkers aren't the ones paying for your retirement, so who cares what they think? Let them laugh if they want; you are too busy generating seed money for your Wealth Wheel to pay attention to what they say.

Option 4: Create income via home-based micro business with no overhead

Another option to start generating more investment capital is by starting a business from home. Specifically, we are talking about something smaller and that provides an almost immediate flow of cash. For example, think about running a simple home-based business. Let me take a moment to clear something up: When I talk about a home-based business, I am not talking about a job. I don't want you to focus on being someone else's employee, just on working from your home. Many people think of being a virtual assistant, or doing data entry, as the only option for earning money from home. While those *are* ways to make extra money which you *could* consider, what I am talking about here is using your imagination to find ways of making money but without investing money, dealing with a boss, or having to purchase much office equipment. Most of my ideas here can be done with a computer and access to the Internet, something you probably already have.

Do you enjoy gardening and are you a good writer? Write a special report on gardening and sell it online. Are you a good writer, and could you do independent writing assignments from home? A friend of mine falls into this category. He lives in the Dominican Republic, yet he is a U.S. citizen. He writes for a living from his home. He writes about everything from real estate articles to health reports; he even does some editing. He has no overhead; he only has a computer and Internet access. He communicates with his customers through e-mail and Skype. They pay him via PayPal. He is happy, and they are happy. If you are a good writer, you can do the same.

Another idea would be something like selling products using online auction sites or your own website. Do you like buying stuff on eBay? How about selling stuff professionally (or as a part-time job)? How would you like to sell on eBay without ever having to ship anything? After finding out what a wholesaler has for sale, you can simply list them online. Then, after the auction, you can pass the order on to the supplier and have the supplier drop ship it directly to the purchaser. By becoming the middle man, you have made money without having to invest any money up front and without having to store inventory in your house or make trips to the post office.

One of the many cool things about eBay is that you can preschedule auctions for any time during the week, so you can create them in your free time at night and on the weekends and then they run on their own while you are at your full-time job. The system is automated, which allows you to get the maximum amount of money for your time invested.

Are you a good project manager? Are you good at taking a variety of tasks and forming them into a checklist? Can you coordinate teams of people and make sure that everyone knows what they have to do and how to do it? There are people and companies out there who might hire you to coordinate events and projects for them. From weddings to job fairs to community picnics in the park, someone has to be in charge of making sure things go smoothly, and that could be you. Along with local listings, check job posting websites like elance.com and craigslist.org for job postings. As a matter of fact, there is an entire online marketing industry where many people are looking for qualified Joint Venture Managers who can coordinate cooperation projects between different online marketers for a fee or for a percentage of sales.

Here's another high-powered suggestion if you have established the reputation of being a trustworthy person and have access to a network of people who have some money to invest: Offer to invest their money in high-yielding tax lien certificates (TLC) that pay 16–36 percent interest on the investments. Offer to do these investments for others for a fee or in exchange for keeping a percentage of the interest. If you don't know what a tax lien is, a TLC is an option offered by counties across the country to collect property taxes. They place a lien on the property and then sell the lien at auction. The winner gets paid the property taxes owed, plus the interest. By setting yourself up as the middle man, you can get either a flat fee or a percentage. If the TLC offers 16 percent interest, offer to give them 12 percent; you keep 4 percent just for doing the work. This can be a great way to make some money in the short term. Plus, those who invest get a great return on their investment, and it was no money out of your pocket. Just make sure you follow all the Federal Trade Commission rules when offering to do this for others. Not only can you make this a profitable business, but you soon can start investing in your own TLC which give you great Temporary Cash Flow. To find out more about tax lien investing, one of my personal areas of expertise, you can go to www.ForeverCash.com/tlc.

Another great business that you can run from your home office is, of course, real estate investing—the vehicle that allowed me to make some quick money that I later reinvested in Temporary Cash and Forever Cash. First, you need to look at the different types of real estate investment types and decide what you would like to do:

- Fix and flip
- Short sales
- Land flips
- Note buying and private money lending
- Wholesaling
- Be a landlord
- Single family vs. multifamily vs. retail vs. office. All have their own rules and pros and cons.
- Tax liens and/or tax deeds
- Probate investing (buying real estate out of probate)
- Mobile home investments

Each technique is a great way to make the seed money you need in a short time; sometimes, it's as short as a few weeks. If you are new to the world of real estate investing, take the time to educate yourself first. For many—like land flipping and wholesaling—you don't even need to have money to make money. There are many ways to use your brain instead of your pocketbook to make profits in real estate. Find the deal, lock it up, and pass it on to someone else.

To learn more about these ways of investing, go to www.ForeverCash. com/realestate.

Option 5: Use the Internet

If you are not interested in starting an offline home-based business or getting a part-time job, consider how you can use the Internet to make money. The conventional wisdom was always "you need money to make money." While it is true that you need a certain amount of seed money to purchase your Forever Cash Assets, you should never think that unless you win the lottery or get a huge bonus that you are doomed to a life of poverty. With the Internet, it has never been easier to make money without investing anything beyond the price of the computer and the Internet connection that you already have.

Here are a few suggestions:

Consider becoming an affiliate marketer. An affiliate marketer is someone who makes money selling other people's stuff on the Internet. It is the way most professional Internet marketers have started their careers. You don't need a website; you don't need a product; and you don't need a list of subscribers. All you need to know is how to find buyers and send them to other people's online product offers. You find an online product you can believe in, and you can match interested people up with the offer you have found online via channels like Facebook, online forums, or a simple web group search (all free). Each time someone buys the product, you get paid a commission by the owner of the product.

I know a person who set up multiple Twitter accounts, including one for each of his two dogs (something that *officially* Twitter doesn't allow, but then again Twitter did not check). Using some free tools, he built up large followings of over 10,000 people for each of these accounts. At the same time, he searched for cheap products having to do with dogs and dog care that had affiliate programs. Then, he would tweet about them from his dog's Twitter account—I am not making this up—using an affiliate link. Results? The last time I talked to him he was making about $5,000 a month in commissions referring obvious dog-loving people over to these commission-paying products – from his dogs' Twitter accounts. If a *dog* can make $5,000 a month part-time, I think we humans should be able to do that, too! It can be done without *any* money on your part, and you never deal with processing payments or storing inventory, and yet you get paid. In some cases, the seller will give you a significant percentage of the price (up to 100 percent of the customer's first purchase).

Or, consider investing in book royalties. While you may not fancy yourself an author, you can still get a piece of the eBook pie. How? After doing some research to find out what kinds of books are selling, get in touch with a ghostwriter online (using the aforementioned online communities of craigslist.com and elance.com) to set up a deal to write a high-quality book or special report. After you have the final version of the book, just self-publish the book on Amazon.com, which has a database of millions of credit card-carrying customers eager to download your book. You can receive royalties off each digital copy sold, and your out-of-pocket expense is minimal. Book sales are great, and they do provide passive and recurring income. However, sales will eventually slow down and maybe stop altogether. The key is then to either keep writing more books, or to collect the Temporary Cash Flow, not spend it, and reinvest it into a different Forever Cash Asset.

Along with selling goods online, there is also the option of selling your services. The technological era has made it possible that clients and contractors can collaborate on projects even though they are separated by national and cultural boundaries. What are some services that you may be able to sell online? One of the people who works on some of my websites is a programmer from Russia. We have never met; we have never spoken to each other in person or even via Skype. We just write e-mails back and forth, and he does the programming work we ask him to do. He is based in Russia; we are based in the United States. The Internet makes it possible. Do you love doing online work? Are you good when working with software like WordPress, PHP, Java or know how to write apps for the Apple or Droid systems? There is always a need for a good programmer, WordPress designer, and for anyone who can make the client's vision a reality.

Think about this: Do you have a great voice? There is always a need for voiceovers in the age of YouTube and other video-sharing websites all over the Internet. News organizations, companies, and private blogs are all looking for people to help them get their message across. On websites like voices.com, jobs are posted and interested people can audition for the role. Think about it: You can provide the voice for a television commercial, a cartoon, or even a documentary—all from the comfort of your home office.

Promoting your services online can even take you in a more creative direction. Are you an artist? Can you create interesting designs and layouts on your computer? Can you convey even abstract ideas and thoughts using your electronic paintbrush? Lots of people are looking for graphic designers, logo designers, and people who can make their brand come to life. On elance.com, 99designs.com, fiverr.com, and other places, you can get paid by the job for doing something that you already love. All across the Internet. Making the seed money that you need has never been more fun!

The bottom line is this: There are many ways to make more money. Only if you already have a high-paying position would you want to focus more on cutting your expenses to provide for the cash you need to get financially free. Everyone else needs to find ways to make as much *seed* money as possible so that you can turn it into Forever Cash.

Chapter 12

HOW THE RICH THINK OF TIME: THE TIME HORIZON

How important is getting out of the hamster wheel of financial hell or the earn-to-spend cycle for you?

You might not think that money is the most important thing in life, and I agree to some degree, but it sure makes all the most important things in life more enjoyable. I have seen too many married couples drift apart as they work day and night just to pay the bills. All they do is work, work, work to just pay the bills and buy some toys, and they don't ever have time for each other. You know these couples, too. You see them getting divorced. They didn't get divorced because of a lack of money; they got divorced because lack of money caused fights all the time. I have also seen how couples have to get reacquainted with each other after finally retiring because they hardly spent any time together during the previous thirty years. I have seen too many fathers spending weeks away from their families at their jobs, only to come home to kids who hardly know them. I have seen too many people trapped in an 8-to-5 job they don't like, working with people they don't particularly care for, and how—despite their sacrifices—they are barely able to pay the bills and still feel terrified about the future. As a matter of fact, the vast majority of all marital fights could be resolved if the subject of money could be taken care of once and for all.

- Don't like how your spouse cleans the house or you and/or your spouse don't like cleaning the house? A maid would help that instantly.
- The schools in your area are bad? Having money to be able to move into a better area or send your kid to a good private school would fix that.
- Your car is constantly breaking down or you don't have a car? Money would fix that.
- Bills stacking up at home? Money will also fix that.
- Have your mother-in-law moving in, and you can't stand her? With money, you can buy her a separate house or condo so that you are close by but not on top of each other.

Think about what you fight about at home. Aren't most of those subjects of debate about topics that money could fix? *That* is why money is so important. We all make a bunch of money every year through our jobs, right? Unfortunately, most people have nothing to show except piles of junk and receipts. Yet, it's a totally different thing to keep and grow what you make. It's important to be able to retire without ever having to be afraid that the money will disappear and go "poof" in a cloud of smoke, like it did for many people who invested in the stock market at the wrong time.

I have been trying to help you develop a new mindset, a new way of thinking. Instead of thinking the way that you have been programmed to think by the financial industry who only has its own interests in mind and the media members who get their paychecks from the big investment corporations, I want you to see the world the way that the truly wealthy see it. I want you to make financial decisions the same way they do. As I mentioned earlier, I am a fan of looking at the people who are successful in a certain area of their life and asking them how they got there and what the secret is.

One secret I have learned in speaking with wealthy individuals has to do with the way that they view their goals and the time it takes to reach them. The rich work while keeping the big picture in mind. In other words, they are always thinking of the long-term consequences of their actions. With almost every financial decision they make, they ask themselves "how will this affect my overall financial goals? If I spend this money, will it bring me closer or take me further away from where I want to go?"

The rich recognize the value of every single dollar spent. For example, take the following quote from Kevin O'Leary, a Canadian venture capitalist featured on the television program *Shark Tank* on ABC. He has a definitive way of looking at his money. He says:

"Money is my military. Each dollar, a soldier. I never send my money into battle unprepared and undefended. I send it to conquer and take currency prisoner and bring it back to me."[6]

That is how the rich think. Instead of just asking whether they want a certain toy, or whether they can afford to do something, they ask themselves what effect this purchase or investment will have on their future. And if they see that it will not help them, or that it will even harm them, then they won't spend the money. The truly wealthy people of the world have learned the secret of delayed gratification.

Do you remember the Stanford marshmallow experiment I mentioned earlier? The children who were able to wait all the way until the researchers came back were rewarded with an extra marshmallow. Those who couldn't wait missed out. The truly wealthy have learned to wait for that second marshmallow. Actually, they have mastered the game to the point where—by the end of the day—they own the entire bag of marshmallows that magically gets filled up each month again without them doing anything for it anymore. They have seen the advantages of saying no to certain toys now to invest in cash-producing assets. Using the cash flow from those assets, they can buy the toy later on (heck, they can probably buy ten of them). The rich adjust their daily decisions based on their overall goals.

Let's look at an example. A rich person might find himself at a car dealership thinking about purchasing that 2013 Mercedes. With its beautiful lines and new car smell, a weaker person might just fork over every dime he has to drive that car off the lot. Or, worse yet, he might get up to his ears in debt to pay for it. How would a rich person handle that situation?

A rich person would start by classifying the asset, in this case, as something that will go down in value and in addition, if financed, take money out of their pocket each month. The rich person will ask himself if purchasing this new car will set him back in his financial goals and will take him further away from achieving his goal of financial freedom. If it will have a negative effect on his goals, he will walk away without thinking twice.

On the other hand, if—for whatever reason—he finds himself without a car and feels that not owning a vehicle is holding him back financially, then purchasing a vehicle will actually help him to reach his goals. It would be in harmony with the big picture for him to get a car. However, then the other question after that is "does it have to be a new $50,000 Mercedes?" or "can it be a two-year-old Mercedes for $35,000," or even "a four-year-old Toyota Camry for $15,000?" All are reliable, all of them look good, and all will most likely get the job of getting you from point A to point B done without breaking down. All will set you back financially by having to take money out of your pocket. Each, however, will have a different impact on how much they set you back and therefore how quickly or how slowly you reach your goal.

Perhaps he already owns a Mercedes but the car is now five years old, and he is considering a replacement. Should he replace it because the factory warranty just expired, and he is afraid the repairs will start adding up (German car repairs are expensive), or should he just buy an extended warranty for a few thousand dollars and instead take the money a new car would have cost and buy more Forever Cash Flow assets with it? After all, once the Mercedes does need to be replaced down the road, the Forever Cash Flow assets would be able to pay for the full monthly payment of a new car. Once it's paid off, the cash would still continue to come in—forever paying for another new car and another one and another one…

I won't tell you which one to buy. That decision depends on where you are in the process of getting to your financial goal. Perhaps you already have several thousand dollars a month in passive Forever Cash coming into your bank accounts, and you have other *active* income streams that bring in a lot more than that. In that case, the most expensive car is probably fine (although I personally *never* buy new cars; I always buy them when they are one to two years old).

Until the truly generationally wealthy have an abundance of cash coming in from Forever Cash sources, they truly always judge any expense against what it could do for them if allowed to compound and be invested again and again and again for a few years. That's the goal: Be aware of what each chunk of money spent means to your financial future, and what effect—positive or negative—it will have on your goals.

The wealthy also understand that building wealth is not something that happens overnight. We do live in an instant gratification world, and people don't look at the process it takes to generate wealth but only at the event that generated the wealth, like the sale of a company. They forget to think of the hard work and the disciplined process that it took to get there. No self-made millionaire or cash-flow millionaire did it overnight. Sorry I had to burst your bubble, but it just doesn't happen like that in the real world.

What does happen is that successful entrepreneurs and investors prepare for success for years by studying, getting educated, making lots of mistakes, and learning from them. Once the opportunity presents itself, they will then have the tools, the relationships, the knowledge, and—ideally—the experience to pull off the feat and to make a ton of money in a short time. Once they have made some money, they know not to squander it. Instead, they invest it again and again to make more money and ultimately to invest that money in cash flow assets. Unlike the celebrities we saw earlier who blew tens of millions of dollars on extravagant houses, parties, vacations, and jewelry, the Forever Cash Assets ensure that both they, their children, and—hopefully—even their grandchildren and beyond, will be set forever. You can see that again and again and again if you look for them. The problem is the truly generationally Forever Cash wealthy don't usually show up in the media. They live more silent yet highly profitable and highly abundant lives.

There is a saying: "Most people vastly overestimate what they can do in one year and vastly underestimate what they can do in five or ten years."

The passing of time can achieve results with our money that, in our own power, we could never hope to attain. Let's look again at how the rich avoid foolish spending by thinking of all that money might accomplish. Let's say that a rich person decided to buy the four-year-old Toyota Camry for his son's sixteenth birthday instead of the shiny new Mercedes. While the kid might not be thrilled, the father will have saved approximately $35,000. What can the father achieve using that $35,000 with the passage of time? Let's say that, for whatever reason, the father chooses not to invest in a Forever Cash Asset, but instead puts the money into a high-return investment like tax liens. Let's say that this account pays the impressive rate of 10 percent per year (actually, most tax liens pay between 14–36 percent, so this is super conservative).

What happens as time passes? The magic of compound interest. Have you ever heard this term before? Compound interest is a straightforward concept: It is an amount of money that is deposited into a financial institution, and the depositor receives a certain percentage of interest. Now, at the end of each year, the depositor has a choice. He can withdraw the interest earned or leave it in the account. If he leaves it, then the interest becomes part of the principal amount and starts to earn interest itself. The next year goes by, he now earns interest on a greater amount, and the amount keeps increasing.

The growth is impressive. After twenty years of 10 percent growth, that initial $35,000 saved by not buying that 2013 Mercedes will have grown to more than $235,462.50. After thirty years, it is $610,729.08; and after forty years, it is $1,584,073.94.

Would you still like to get the $35,000 Mercedes if you knew it could cost you $1.5 million over forty years? What do you think Junior would prefer in the big scheme of things?

The rich have learned to see the big picture for every dollar they spend. They recognize the potential of even seemingly small purchases and transactions to carry them closer or push them further away from their financial goals. That is the way that you have to learn to think as well, every minute of every day. While in particular I want you to learn this new way of looking at money, this principle can be applied much more broadly. You see, you are in the asset allocation business. Along with your money, you have several other types of assets that need to be distributed out throughout your day and your life in order to achieve the most success. Among your personal assets are:

- Your time
- Your energy
- Your attention

Even though I am in the education business, *and* the real estate business, *and* the marketing business, all of these sectors are part of the asset allocation business. Be like the wealthy. Learn to spend your money by keeping the big picture in mind. Ask yourself with each purchase: Is this going to get me closer to my goal? Then, take your assets and put them to the best use.

Chapter 13

GOOD INVESTMENTS VS. BAD INVESTMENTS

The previous chapters went into depth about what exactly the Wealth Wheel principle is all about and how the rich think. These principles are exciting, once you get them working for you. Now let's talk about what to invest this money in, once you make it.

The main reason people lose their mountains of money is that they don't know how to tell a good investment from a bad one. Most people don't even know when to call a purchase an investment versus an expense. Even if they do an investment, they don't know how to maximize their investments.

They say things like this:

- I invested in this car.
- I invested in this 401k.
- This haircut was a good investment.
- I invested in a pool.

But are these *really* investments? Or are these expenses that bring you no return?

I want to introduce a better term, and that is the term of "asset." An asset is anything that has value, including the old clothes in your closet, all the way up to your house, and also any investments that bring cash flow every month. So almost everything you ever buy, own, or will buy is an asset. However, some assets are great assets; some are good assets; some are mediocre assets; some are bad assets; and some assets are horrible. The problem is most people put their money mainly in horrible assets, which should *barely* be called assets. They are expenses that depreciate and are worthless after a while. Yet, they call these things investments. Everyone buys assets all the time. When somebody buys a car, you buy an asset. But that asset happens to go down in value quickly. When somebody buys a stock and that stock goes up, is that a good asset? Most will say, yes, but what if the stock goes down? Is it then a good asset? So whether an asset is great, good, mediocre, bad, or horrible depends on what it does for you, and how its value develops.

What most people spend most of their money on are not even assets but *expenses*. Things like your electricity bill and your car insurance are certainly not assets; they are expenses. Assets are things that contain some value over a longer period. I hope we can agree to that.

Therefore, a car is clearly an asset.

But is it a *good* asset? I would say the answer is a clear "no." It goes down in value and, on top of that, if you have a car payment, necessities like insurance, repair costs, and gas make the cost of owning it go up. It costs serious money to own a car; and each year, it's worth less. That's clearly a bad—if not horrible—asset.

Let's look at your house. This is what most people call their "number-one asset."

And it probably *is* your number-one asset if you have equity in it and if that equity is the biggest amount of value you have, compared to all your other assets.

But let's ask the same question. Is it a *good* asset?

It is certainly better than a car. Over the long run, a house maintains or increases in value.

We all know after the experience of the 2007–2011 real estate market crash that this does not guarantee it will always increase in value. Over the course of the average mortgage of thirty years, however, it usually does at least *keep* its value and most actually go up in value. Yet, at the same time during that entire time until you have paid off your mortgage, you also have to write a monthly check for principle, interest, escrow fee, and property taxes, to be able to live in that house.

So while your house is a better asset than a car, I think it is still not a good asset.

Please notice that I did not say it is not a necessary asset. Everyone needs a place to live in and a roof over their head. If your choice is between renting an apartment for $1,000 or having a $1,000 mortgage, the mortgage is better, because you are building equity in the house over time and, ultimately, will own the house free and clear. It's the better deal. But neither one is an option that gets you closer to financial independence in the short- or mid-term, because both take money from your pocket.

In my book, a house with a mortgage is a bad asset. Once it is paid off, it turns into a good asset. Unless you start renting out rooms to get positive cash flow from the house you live in, it will never be a *great* asset.

So what *is* a good asset?

In my book, the best kind of asset is one that makes you a profit and, at the same time, gives you regular monthly (or quarterly or yearly) cash flow—*forever*. That is my definition of a Forever Cash Asset. It's an asset that goes up in value over time (or at least maintains its value) *and* that gives you cash flow, starting the moment you buy or create it. Examples of that are, cash-flow positive rental real estate, land leases where you lease the land, royalties from books you write, licenses you give out on product inventions, membership fees collected from an online membership website business you create, monthly overrides you receive on the consumption habits of your network marketing down line, and things like that. In all or most of them, the underlying asset, the real estate, the land, the intellectual property for the books, the website, have a value and can be sold for more than it took you to create them or acquire them, and—in all cases—the cash and cash flow coming in over the years pays you *more* than the cost of having bought or created the underlying assets.

That is what you should strive for. That is the Holy Grail of assets.

Yet, what do people spend their money on? Stuff that is completely worthless in a few days, weeks, or years, and on top of that, they put it on their credit cards and therefore end up paying for it for months and years after they stopped using the things they bought. I see it with my tenants all the time. They can just make rent but have every toy under the sun in their houses.

But there are some other asset classes.

The *second* best investment is the kind of investments that throw off Temporary Cash.

They are similar in style in that they also throw off cash flow each month, quarter, or year, but they don't throw off that cash flow stream forever, and the underlying asset does not necessarily go up in value.

For example, if you lend someone $100,000 in an interest-only loan for one year with a 12 percent interest per year, then you receive $1,000 a month in cash-flow profit. At the end of the first year, you also receive the $100,000 back. So your principal was returned, and you made $12,000 in a cash flow, which is all profits. Not too bad! As a matter of fact, deals like that are being made all over the place all the time.

Particularly in the environment of the post-recession years, banks don't easily lend. Many people, particularly investors, are willing to accept higher interest rates from private money lenders to finance their deals. If you have some cash, you can become a private money lender and create cash flow for months, or years, but, ultimately, they will be paid back. And when that happens, your cash flow stops, but you get your principal back and then you just lend it out again and the cash flow starts again.

That is why I call it *Temporary* Cash Flow. It's great, but it doesn't last forever. Because your investment is safe and because you—on top of it—get additional cash flow for a time period, it is still a great asset that is only outscored by the Forever Cash Assets.

Lastly, I want to talk about the other remaining kinds of assets. These assets might go up in value over time, yet they don't take money out of your pocket outside of the initial acquisition cost. Land you hold on to, collectibles, and things like owning currency or stock fall into this category, as well as anything that you buy outright and that has the potential of going up in value. Remember the LEGO story I told you earlier? That would be a classic example of this asset class, too.

These asset classes are often a bit of a gamble *if* you have to buy them at market value or unless you know that market well. They are a great opportunity to increase your seed money if you can buy them with a nice discount off market value and flip them for, or close to, full market value.

Whatever the market value of such an asset does, the fact is that once you own it, it is entirely or almost cost neutral. Once you own a stock of a company, you don't have to spend more money to keep owning it. Once you own a piece of land, you don't have to spend more money to maintain it (other than the property taxes, which I will ignore here because usually they are not that high). Once you own a box of Star Wars LEGO pieces, you don't have to spend more money to keep owning it.

If you bought well—i.e., below market value or with some specific knowledge of how values are expected to develop—you can make a great profit with these kinds of assets.

For example, if you buy a piece of land having seen the city's 10- and 20-year master plan, and you know that you are buying land where the city has plans to build an interstate exit ten years from now, then you have a high probability that your property will go up in value many times by that time. The issue with this asset class is that you don't get closer to quitting your job fast. What I want to focus on is how you can be able to quit your job in a few months or a few years from now, and not ten to twenty years. While you just own that property, you won't get close to that because the property doesn't spit out any cash flow. That is why when I started in the land investing business, I started flipping. Number one, I don't ever buy land at market value, but at 5–25 percent of market value using a specific technique I have developed. Number two, because of that low purchase price, I can flip it fast and often more than double my money in a few days or weeks and do not have to wait ten to twenty years. I only apply this technique of buy-and-hold non-cash-flow properties (which is also called "landbanking") to some of the best properties, which are right in the path of growth and look like they could be worth one hundred times their current value a few years down the road. That multiple of value makes them worth holding onto for longer.

What are dangerous investment classes?

There are some specific investment vehicles that are only offered to you if you already have some money, and if you are an "accredited investor." These are investments in existing businesses or an investment in speculative business projects. While they sound good on paper, it is my recommendation that you stay away from them for now, or if you feel you have to engage in them, that you don't allocate more than 10 percent of your investment money in such speculative investments. Investing $100,000 in a start-up company might sound sexy, but nine out of ten start-ups fail. When that happens, your entire $100,000 is gone. These investments appeal to your inner gambler, the same way the lottery does. The ability to just buy a ticket or, in this case, some shares of a company and without doing anything see it become the next Google or Berkshire Hathaway, making you rich beyond imagination in the process. You know already what my answer is, though. It mostly doesn't happen, so I would rather see you invest your money in something that you know the results upfront and that you can repeat again and again. It is slower; it is more boring, but the results are almost guaranteed.

Only once you have implemented this and have created a life of financial stability and security through Forever Cash, you can take a small portion of your income and invest it in some of these "gambles," and perhaps one will work out and make you even wealthier. But by that time you will have learned much more about business, about finances, and about what is a good opportunity versus a bad one. Right now is not the time for it.

In summary:

- The *best* investments are those that bring in cash flow forever, and, at the same time, go up in value.
- Below "best" are those investments that bring in cash flow for a specific time (months or years) while preserving or paying for the value of the investment with interest.
- Below those are investments that don't provide any cash flow but have the potential for appreciation.
- Below those are investments that have negative cash flow but a *potential* for appreciation.

- Stay away from speculative investment opportunities like start-up investments, unless you know *exactly* what you are doing.
- The *worst* investments are those that are really *not* investments but expenses.

Unfortunately, most people spend all their money on the last category and think it is normal.

Chapter 14

GOOD DEBT
VS. BAD DEBT

I am a 100 percent cash-flow-oriented person. I don't believe that financial security comes from having large amounts of money stored up in bank accounts or stuffed under my mattress; there are too many variables that can make that pile of money disappear. I believe in taking steps to ensure a constant flow of cash each month to my pocket. Like we saw in the previous chapter, the rich don't think immediately about what each dollar can get them. They consider what impact each decision they make will have on their future, whether it will bring them closer to or take them further away from their financial goals.

I do the same thing, in my own way. With each financial decision I make, I ask myself: Will it put money into my pocket or will it take money out of it? This reasoning is not taught in schools or in financial magazines, but it is the key to understanding the difference between good debt and bad debt.

Is that a new concept for you—that there are two types of debt? Some self-proclaimed "financial gurus" will tell you that there is only one type of debt, and that debt is all bad. Others will tell you that debt is power and that you should leverage up to your ears. While I agree that bad debt can certainly bring a lot of harm to anyone, I believe that it is a two-edged sword that can also cut in favor of those holding it. The truth is that debt in itself can be an excellent tool to propel you toward your goal of financial freedom. And it can also destroy you quickly if it is applied excessively in the wrong market environment. What is the difference between good debt and bad debt? Simply put:

- Good debt brings you forward and either creates more cash flow or helps you to create a new windfall of cash which you then use to purchase a cash flow asset.
- Bad debt sucks your cash flow out of your pocket and sets you back financially.

The bottom line when looking at taking on a certain type of debt is simple: Will the debt put money into my pocket and increase my wealth or will the debt take money out and decrease my wealth?

How does a debt *put* money into your pocket?

Such debts do exist. Let's look at a few good debt examples.

We'll start with one of my favorite vehicles for creating cash flow— real estate. How can you use debt to create cash flow? By obtaining a house that you can fix up and then flip for a quick profit. Let's take a moment to crunch the numbers and to see how a debt can put money into your pocket. Imagine that the house that you are looking at is being sold for $100,000. Now, you estimate that it will cost at least

$20,000 for the repairs in maintenance, and that you will be able to sell it afterward for $160,000. With me so far? Good.

But there's a problem: you don't have $120,000 to purchase the house (you only have $20,000) *and* to pay for the repairs. What can you do? You can take out a loan for the missing $100,000. Let's assume the worst-case scenario and imagine that this loan is from a hard money lender, who will probably charge you a stiff fee (up to $10,000 in fees and interest) for that loan. You get the loan, buy the house, fix it up, and are able to sell it for your estimated price of $160,000. You pay back your loan of $110,000 and see that you are left with $30,000 more in your bank account than when you started with. What has just happened? At the beginning of the project, you had $20,000 in your bank account. You invested that money and took on a $100,000 loan which you had to pay back as $110,000. But—at the end of the deal—you had $50,000 in your bank account: a profit of $30,000 for what was possibly just one month's worth of part-time work (if *that*).

House price: $100,000
Repair cost: $20,000
Total investment needed: $120,000
You have in savings: $20,000
Take a hard money loan for: $100,000
Sell the property for: $160,000
Profit: $160,000
- $100,000 for the loan
- $20,000 you put in
- $10,000 land interest and fees
Result: $30,000 in profits for you

Was there a risk? Yes.

Things *could* have gone wrong, and you could have made less or even lost money. Was it a fiscally irresponsible risk? Not at all—and I will tell you why. Even if you had not been able to find a buyer for the house (which was reasonably priced, so it wouldn't have been too difficult), you could still have rented out the house and used the money you received from the renters to pay for the mortgage and *then* some. Even in a worst-case scenario, you would have been able to make that deal work. *Those* are the kind of deals we like.

The housing market got a bad rap as being the primary cause of the recent recession. The problem, however, was never with the houses themselves: It had more to do with the overinflated assessments that were based on *unrealistic* expectations and people's inability to run a simple mortgage calculation. By being educated about these things, my wife and I were able to avoid the financial ruin that so many real estate investors endured after the 2004–2007 housing boom and even *thrive* in the low-priced buyers' market afterward. Let me share another brief example of good debt—the kind of debt that *puts* money into your pocket.

Think of how it might play out if you decided to purchase a small business by utilizing seller financing. As I mentioned in an earlier chapter, seller financing is when the purchaser of a business pays a portion of the sale price up front, and he then makes monthly payments over a set period of time until the rest of the purchase price (and the interest) is paid off. Let's crunch the numbers of what would happen if you invested in a business using seller financing.

Imagine a business that can be managed by you in just four to six hours a week. That business has an asking price of $200,000 and throws off $48,000 a year in cash flow. What are such businesses? They are everywhere—coin laundries, Internet marketing businesses, online membership sites, small self-storage facilities, small franchises, and many other businesses like that. You are interested in purchasing it, but you only have $40,000 to invest. Does that mean you will have to miss this great opportunity? Not if you know how to use the power of good debt—debt that puts money into your pocket. Working with the seller, let's say you agree to a deal like this one:

- You buy the business for the $40,000 in cash you have saved up, and;

- You commit to pay the seller the remaining $160,000 (plus interest) in monthly payments of $2,500 for eight years ($230,000 total).

Now the terms of this deal work for everybody: The seller gets the money he is owed for his business, and you get a Forever Cash Asset. Doesn't that $2,500 a month mean a loss for you? Remember that the business, as is, is throwing off $48,000 per year, or about $4,000 per month. Even after making the payment to the seller, you are left with a positive cash flow of $1,500 per month. The debt that you acquired through seller financing has created a Forever Cash Asset that puts $1,500 into your pocket every month for the next eight years, and $4,000 after that when the business is paid off and 100 percent of the profits come to you!

That means your new business is giving you a 37.5 percent *cash-on-cash return* on your $40,000 investment. It also means that even if you only keep the numbers stable in that business (and don't try to expand it or to make it grow which is, of course, possible), you will have your $40,000 back in a little more than 2.6 years. If you manage the place well, you might be able to double the profits of the store and increase your income and cash flow dramatically. The good debt made that monthly cash flow possible. Without that good debt, you would never have been able to take steps to build that Forever Cash Asset.

Of course, this is a real business probably with employees and overhead, so it might not be the one you want to start with, but it does help illustrate how good debt can help you make more money. As mentioned before, of course debt/leverage is a double-edged sword. It can magnify your gains, but it can also magnify your losses. For example, during the boom, when people invested in houses and leveraged them like crazy, they did not look at cash flow; they only looked at appreciation, and it killed them. When the market turned, all those houses that had been rented out with negative cash flow (with their owners *counting* on appreciation) started to suck their owners dry. Their owners had to pay thousands of dollars more in mortgage payments than they were receiving in rent each month. They were slowly bleeding to death financially. How many houses can you carry when on each of them you lose between $300 and $2,000 a month? Not many.

This happened because of several reasons: People didn't understand the double-edged power of debt; they did not understand what a true investment is; and they did not understand the power of cash flow. Mistake number one was that their "investment" did not generate cash flow in the long run. The second mistake was that they invested in something they bought at market value instead of at a discount. Mistake number three was that they had no idea *if* and *for how much longer* the "investment" would go up in value and counted on the "bigger fool" theory. They failed on three ends.

All through the boom, I was making money by buying pieces of land at a steep discount over market value, selling them at market value, and—on top of it all —offering seller financing and making cash flow that lasts. I never had to ever go to the bank and get a loan. And in the housing arena, I was 100 percent on the sidelines. I did not participate. It didn't make sense to me. Although I didn't know it yet, I had become a *pure cash-flow* investor and, during the days where $1,000-a-month rental houses with $2,000-a-month mortgages were selling for $400,000, buying any of them just didn't make sense to me.

I could not even conceive how people could do such a thing. Everyone out there who was playing that game was just holding out for the next greater fool, who counted on ever-increasing house prices to buy it to just resell it. They all played a game of equity and appreciation, but nobody played the cash flow game. As a result, once the tide turned, all these *big* piles of equity (of funny money or net worth) disappeared quickly, and people lost fortunes. I had never experienced a real estate downturn in my lifetime and, honestly, I didn't and couldn't imagine a downturn of that magnitude, but my conservative nature and the fact that I was primed for cash flow opportunities luckily kept me away from these "investments." They were *not* investments. They were bets—bets that the value of housing would keep going up and up. Although you can get lucky if you snatch the beginning of such a cycle and manage to get out at the top, that is not how you get wealthy predictably. When betting, the house, ultimately, *always* wins. In this case, the house was the last seller and millions of people were left holding the bags. Buying at market price without cash flow and *hoping* is *not* a plan.

Once the prices had fallen low enough, and everyone was scared, the cash flow investors like me came out of the woodwork and started buying up property. At that point, prices had way overshot the goals in the other direction. As a result, the three-bedroom, one-bath houses in decent neighborhoods in Phoenix were available for $26,000. I bought a deal like that, and it rents now for $800 a month, giving me a good $500 in monthly cash flow (even after taking into consideration a small mortgage). Another house I invested in is more than 2,000 square feet, five bedrooms and three baths. I paid $40,000 for it ($20 per square foot). It rents for $1,050 a month, also giving me a good $600 in positive cash flow each month, even after subtracting the repairs, property taxes, rental taxes, and mortgage. We bought more houses in that time period, and I keep buying right now because the numbers make sense. Actually, I bought most of these houses with *cash* and then went and refinanced them so I could leverage my cash even more and buy more and build more cash flow.

I do believe, however, that there is such a thing as too much leverage. Too much leverage is just as dangerous as buying too high. If you have a $1,000 mortgage and receive $1,050 in rent, I don't like that deal because with one missed payment, you are bleeding financially. As long as you can buy houses for $40,000, $60,000, or even up to $100,000 at the current low interest rates with a 30-year fixed rate, you can leverage them up to 100 percent, if you can find a lender willing to finance it, and you will still have a nice cash flow. Even at those numbers, that was never my style. I am at the core a truly conservative person, and I subscribe to Warren Buffett's financial rules one and two. Rule one is to never lose money, and rule two is to never forget rule one.

I am deeply aware of what bad debt or too much leverage can cause. *That* is financial distress. If you have a loan/mortgage against your assets, that loan payment has to be paid first each month before you get paid.

So while I like good debt, particularly for real estate, I do keep my loan-to-value ratios low, meaning I never go out and borrow 100 percent of the asset value. As a matter of fact, I don't even go close to that number.

I personally am okay with financing 50–70 percent of the asset value to the limit of having my mortgage payment be up to 50 percent of my monthly rent income. That's the same for a business as it is for real estate. That means I have a $100,000 house and that I am only putting a $50,000– $70,000 loan against that house with a monthly payment no higher than half of the rent. If I have a $500,000 business I only place a $250,000 business loan against it, and use that money to improve the business. A 50 percent loan-to-value ratio or having mortgage payments of only 50 percent of what you take in rents to me means that 50 percent of my houses can be vacant (something that *never* happens), and I still can make my mortgage payment just from the cash flow of the other 50 percent occupied houses. A 50 percent business loan means that the business can operate at *below* capacity, and you still make money and have a *positive* income. It's an additional buffer of safety. While the 50–70 percent loan-to-value ratio is a somewhat arbitrary number, it came from me turning on my brain and asking myself, "What are you comfortable with?" While it financially would be better to take on a higher loan, I sleep better at night knowing that even if things would fall apart and up to 50 percent of my houses are empty, I would still be making enough cash flow to pay the mortgages.

Because I only leverage them conservatively, all my houses are cash flow positive. Because I don't need the cash my houses generate to live for myself, I can use the cash flow they produce for new investments in more cash flow properties, *or* I can take the cash flow and use it to pay down the mortgages on these houses—so that they are soon free and clear and cash flow even more.

The great thing about this type of low debt, especially in real estate spitting out Forever Cash, is that it rarely comes back to harm you, because you are not dependent on property values. For as long as you don't sell the property, it doesn't matter if the house goes up by 200 percent or goes down by 50 percent. You still will make the same or similar cash flow.

If another real estate bubble was to happen or another crash, I honestly would not care. My cash flow would not be affected in any material form. Actually, after the last crash in home prices and the following foreclosure wave, in many areas rental rates went up 10–20 percent while real estate prices were down 40–60 percent or even more. Why? Because all the people who lost their houses during the crisis still needed to have a place to live in, they flooded the rental market. If more people need rental homes, rent goes up. At the same time, buying a house as an investment became something nobody wanted to do anymore, which drove prices even further down.

As someone who follows the masses, that is a problem. For someone who is a contrarian and goes against the masses, this is the definition of paradise—paradise in form of lower prices and higher rents. It's just a matter of how you look at the world.

Can you see how this can boost your cash flow and your return on investment? You didn't have to and still don't have to time the market. As long as you buy the property, such that it cash flows sufficiently at the price you bought it at, and you don't sell the property in a downturn, you are doing great and can expect to ride out any period of lower values while getting the same (or increasing) cash flow from the property.

With this scenario, you do need to learn how to manage the tenants or—better—manage the property managers, but that is easy. For example, we have a property manager who manages our properties and—while that costs us $75 per month per property—all we need to do is call him once or twice a month to check on the rent collection and to make sure if we have a vacancy he is after it and filling it quickly, but that takes about two hours a month. The rest of the month I don't have to worry about it and certainly don't have to go to a job to work forty hours a week for less income.

Let's review: What is the difference between good debt and bad debt? Bad debt is incurred when you get something that will not increase your cash flow. In most cases, this includes the mortgage on the house you live in and your car payment, along with all consumer debt. Good debt is the debt that puts money in your pocket and makes you wealthier. Before you borrow another dime, ask yourself: Is this a good debt or a bad debt?

Chapter 15

DON'T CUT UP
YOUR CREDIT CARDS

ave you ever been to a car race like a Formula 1 or NASCAR—
or even just a horse race? What do they all have in common?
No idea? Let me tell you. Their vehicles (or animals) are as
light as possible. Every ounce of extra weight is being removed to make
them faster. Whether it's Formula 1 or NASCAR, the cars are made
not from steel anymore but from fiberglass or another high-tech, super-
lightweight material. Any extra piece in that car that is not absolutely
needed is removed. The same is true for horse racing. Have you seen
the saddles used for the race? They are tiny and weigh a fraction of the
more-traditional saddle. Have you seen the jockeys? They are also tiny

and often weigh close to 100 pounds. Saddle and rider are selected so that the horse has to carry the least possible weight. Excess weight, of course, slows them down.

The exact same scenario applies to your path to financial security, independence, and freedom from a job forever. As I mentioned before, I do not think you should cut your credit cards up and deprive yourself of all the nice things that life has to offer only to reach a financial goal and get to a place that you think will bring you happiness. I believe you should enjoy the journey getting to that place. There is no joy in accomplishing something if you have to deprive yourself of everything that you enjoy. Yet, there is a clear benefit to reducing expenses, because it speeds up the process of breaking the hamster wheel of financial hell.

The fastest, most-effective, and most-reliable path to financial security goes through playing offense and defense at the same time. You must generate more cash, but you also need to make sure the cash you make is used wisely and doesn't increase your worthless expenses. The fewer expenses you have to carry, the faster you can proceed.

Do you want to speed up the process? The answer to the question of how long it will take to be financially secure and independent hinges on two factors.

- How much extra money can you generate (that can be used to invest)?
- How many expenses do you need to cover with Forever Cash?

What expenses can you get rid of without suffering too much and losing the joy of the process?

When I talk about how many expenses we need to cover with Forever Cash, basically I am talking about your monthly budget. *Where* you live and *how* you live are what determine this number. For example, according to NakedApartments.com, if you live in New York City, the rent for an average two-bedroom in Manhattan is more than $4,000 a month. Yet, in other parts of the world this is quite different. Remember Mike, the writer I mentioned earlier? He lives modestly in the Dominican Republic and spends most of his time as a volunteer working on humanitarian projects; his expenses are low. In fact, I was shocked to discover that he and his wife live comfortably on only $500 a month! For him, just one or two Forever Cash Assets each spitting out $500 a month would provide more than he needs, and more would technically make him financially independent and free.

Every person's circumstances are different, and so their goals have to be different. Mike uses online writing as his vehicle to earn seed money, and after he learned about these concepts, he planned to invest in e-books and in a small business—specifically, a batting cage for the local kids that will satisfy the local population's love of baseball and earn him some passive income. Then, he will be able to focus on his volunteer work without worrying about his finances.

That's the point: The Forever Cash that covers more than your monthly expenses gives you the ability to live your life doing what you want, without worrying about money.

The lower your expenses are, the faster things will go. Within a short time, a few cheap rental houses, along with a small online business or a network marketing position, will bring in more cash flow than you are spending.

If you have huge monthly expenses, yet you barely have any Forever Cash income coming in, you are depending on your active income. To break free, you either have to build up a huge amount of Forever Cash or first have to work on lowering the expense part while you ramp up the income part. That will take a little time; therefore, things will move more slowly, particularly at the beginning until you have reduced expenses. Again, I am not telling you to cut up your credit cards, to lose the iPad, not to go on vacation. But you want to be aware of the relationship between expenses and the speed at which you are proceeding. The more ongoing unnecessary expenses you have, the longer it will take to get to your goal.

Let's return to that NASCAR analogy. Think about yourself like being on a NASCAR racetrack. Not always the most powerful car wins.

Often, the car wins that has good power and low weight. A tow truck would have no chance ever to win a NASCAR race. It has a powerful engine, but it is pulling three cars, and the tow truck alone is super heavy. Are you a race car that is powerful *and* lean, or a tow truck full of expenses that drag you down? The more unuseful expenses you have, the more you are like a tow truck with no chance to ever succeed. That's how it is for cars. Modern race cars obviously need some pieces, like a powerful engine (your ability to play offense, and move forward and create cash), a steering wheel and dashboard (your education), gas, seats, fenders, benders, tires, and other things like that. But a race car doesn't need seat heaters, Christmas reindeer antlers, eighteen cup holders, and four iPhone plugs… and it certainly doesn't need to pull three cars, a house, and other ballast. Neither do you. In the race car world, every ounce of weight counts.

The analogy could not be more perfect. One of the cars we have as a family is a little Mini Cooper convertible. My wife, daughter, and I love driving that little bubble open on a nice spring day. It has far less power than the BMW, but you know what? It is just as fast and accelerates just as quickly. Why? The Mini only has a V4 Engine; the BMW, a V8

Engine. The Mini only has about 170 horsepower while the BMW has about 350 horsepower.

Why is there no noticeable difference?

Because the Mini doesn't weigh anything. The little engine it has only needs to pull 2,800 pounds.

The BMW needs to pull over around 5,000 pounds. Although the BMW is much stronger, it has to pull a much heavier load. It's not always about the power of the engine; it's also about the load you are carrying.

That's what I meant earlier on when I said that if you have less income right now and live a lower expense lifestyle you might have an advantage over someone who already lives a million dollar lifestyle. You have to cover less expense to break out of the hamster wheel of earn-to-spend and transition into the world of having all your expenses covered by Forever Cash. You need less Forever Cash to accomplish your goals.

Keep that in mind when moving forward. Think about every expense you have as something that slows you down on your way to financial independence. The more such useless weight you have the slower you will be able to go and the longer it will take to get there.

Another analogy is that each monthly expense creates a hole you have to dig yourself out of. The more expenses you have, the deeper the hole becomes, and—logically—the fewer such expenses you have, and the more bills you have paid off, the shallower the hole and the less income you need to live your dream lifestyle.

Imagine having a $10,000-a-month lifestyle with a $5,000 mortgage, $3,000 in car payments and credit cards, and $1,000 in gas, insurance, utilities, and so on. You actually don't have that much money left each month. You are trapped in a golden cage and to keep your life the same, you have to generate $10,000 a month in Forever Cash to be safe.

If you managed to reduce your mortgage to $4,000 by refinancing at a lower rate and by paying down the mortgage, and if you pay off your credit cards as well as your cars, then that only adds up to $4,000 per month in expenses or about $5,000 less than in the first scenario.

You need to either generate $5,000 less in extra income to cover that same lifestyle, driving the same cars and living in the same house, or if you still generated $10,000 in extra income each month, you have an extra $5,000 to apply to your seed money to invest in more Forever Cash Assets. In this example, once you reached $5,000 a month in income from your Forever Cash investments, you are financially safe. The bottom line is that by lowering your expense load in a smart way, and by following the Wealth Wheel process, you can have the *same* lifestyle, but you need to earn much less.

The fastest way to get there is:

- Stop digging yourself deeper into the expense hole.
- Increase your earnings as quickly as you can and use some of that to get out of the debt spiral.

Deprivation is not the key. If any financial advice is not enjoyable, it is perceived as difficult. If it is difficult, then people won't keep it up long-term, and they will eventually fail. It's like going on a diet to lose weight long-term. Long-term diets just don't work. What does work is doing a little bit of the diet, cutting out the worst foods most of the time and the bad foods (but not as bad as the worst) many times (equals playing defense by reducing the bad elements) but counteract that with physical activity to burn more calories (equals playing offense by actively burning more calories). What's required is not a diet, but a lifestyle change.

It's the same here. If you cut up your credit cards, get rid of your cell phone, sell your Mercedes and buy a twenty-year-old rusty Chevy, move from your nice apartment to a shack in a dangerous neighborhood, and instead of eating out four times a week you cut it to once per month, you will absolutely be able to save a lot of money. You will probably save a few thousand dollars a month easily, which you can apply to your investments. It takes a special kind of person, however, to be able to do that. It is not the path for most of us. Chances are that you will feel miserable living like that. You will feel like all the life juice is being sucked out of you.

You could opt to go longer term but simpler:

- Change your cell phone provider or change to a cheaper plan.
- Check to see if changing cable provider will save you money.
- Check to see if you can get a higher deductible on your car, if you are a safe driver.
- Adjust the house thermostat when you leave the house.
- Keep your car a few more years once it's paid off.
- If it is not paid off, think about trading it in (if you have equity in it) for something that is good-looking *and* that you can pay for with cash from your car equity.

And if you are up for it and take this seriously, you might want to look into making some more serious self-evaluations:

- Do you even need a third car?
- Do you need to live in a four-bedroom house alone? Or can you get a roommate to help reduce the cost of having the house?

A friend of ours just bought a house that costs him $1,200 a month. He found two roommates who each pay close to $450, meaning our friend just has to cover $300 per month to break even. Yet, he gets tax benefits and the increasing equity in the house. If he had a four-bedroom house, he could rent out one more room, and with that he could make his own house cash flow at $150 per month. With that, he would have turned a lower-quality asset into the best kind of asset, a Forever Cash Asset that goes up in value and provides cash flow.

Getting in financial control of your life is not just about cutting up credit cards; it is about managing your money *differently*. Getting out of bad debt, particularly consumer debt and credit card debt, is one of the most crucial items you want to make part of your plan. Debt carried over from one month is not only expensive, but—if you miss a few payments—it also means extra fees, expenses, and a lower credit score. A lower credit score will, in turn, make it more difficult to get good rates on mortgages. So an important part of taking the defense has to do with paying off your credit cards and card loans. It is one of the most important parts of your strategy which you can start attacking today. They strangle you if you don't.

Where can you start if you feel overloaded with debt? Pay off your credit cards with this specific method.

- List all your credit cards on a sheet with their balances and interest rates.
- Sort them. Start with the one that has the lowest balance and end with the one that has the highest balance and ignore their interest rates.
- List how much you pay toward your credit cards each month. Chances are you are paying more toward them than just the minimum amounts. Chances are if you are like most people, you pay the most extra money to the one you owe the most on. You will stop that now.
- Pay just the minimum payment on all of them except for the one that you owe the least on from now on. On *that* one, you will pay as much as possible.
- Apply as much of a bonus payment on top of the minimum payment on that first lowest balance credit card as possible each month. This method allows you to pay that one off quickly (usually within three to five months).
- That will give you a boost of excitement and motivation.
- Take the large payment you had been paying to that first credit card that is now no longer applied, and roll it over to the credit card with the second-lowest balance, in addition to the minimum payment you are making on that card. This will start paying that second-lowest credit card balance down quickly and actually even faster, because now you in effect are making two

    minimum payments, plus a bonus payment on this one, until
    you pay that one off.

- Take the total monthly boosted payment you made toward the second credit card, and roll that over to the third card until it is paid off, and then to the fourth and the fifth and to the car loans and furniture loans, etc.

This process is called the Debt Snowball method. It is a popular way to eliminate debt advertised by many good financial advisors as well as some financial TV and radio hosts.

Can you see how with that you start paying off card after card and car after car ever faster? It's like magic! Each card that is paid off and each loan that is paid off is a little confidence booster that you can do this and that you are making progress. In addition, all of that also increases your credit score and prepares you for being able to borrow good debt; the one that will help set you free.

Something exciting starts to happen here. Money starts to shift in the way it flows through your life, like the tide coming in. Instead of watching all your hard-earned money fly out the window each month in stupid expenses, you watch payment after payment go down to zero. As you take control of your finances, and win bad debt victory after victory, you start also using some of that money to create your seed money for the Wealth Wheel process by putting it into that separate seed money investment account. Now the real fun starts. As the Wealth Wheels start generating money for you, and you have less going out in unnecessary expenses, you start to feel turbocharged in your financial life, and you start feeling how it is to own your own life and to be in charge of your future. You start seeing the light at the end of the tunnel.

Remember that one of the points of this book is to help you to keep from falling back into the old habits. Expenses and overhead tend to creep up as we go through life. You get the new iPad, and with it you end up paying up to $30 per month for a data plan. Because you rarely use your iPad outside the house, you probably won't even notice the difference if you cancel that plan and instead just use the Wi-Fi you most likely already have in your house to access the Internet. *Bam!* You have saved $30 a month, totaling $360 a year! If you reduce your expenses in a sensible way without affecting your lifestyle a lot, you now feel good and —at the same time—have made it much easier to get out of the hamster wheel of earning to spend. Remember, each dollar you have already committed for overhead expenses is a dollar that cannot be used for investing. But if you eliminate that expense, you can use the dollar you just worked for to invest and forever generate income for you.

Lower your load and increase your income to truly turbocharge your progress.

If you want it badly enough, then cutting out your current unnecessary expenses and bad expenses will be easy, because they will give you a feeling of progress toward your goal. I know of a person who, upon discovering this relationship between expenses and speed of progress, literally sold his 4,000-square-foot custom home in Scottsdale and moved into a one-bedroom apartment to save thousands a month in expenses and to be able to apply that cash toward his path out of debt and into financial independence. While he probably misses the comforts, he is experiencing joy from of the progress he is making in his financial life. The best part about this is that in probably just three to five years, he will be able to buy a similar large house again—but this time in cash—and this time; it will be from the money that his Forever Cash throws off. That is the power of delayed gratification and knowing when to carry a low load. Yet, this drastic change is not for everyone, and it doesn't have to be. If you are less committed to having a number of worldly things that lose value and that is important to you, you will still arrive at your goal; it will just take a bit longer but probably be more enjoyable.

Slashing expenses is particularly important if you consider quitting your job and jumping into this Wealth Wheel method to generate Forever Cash Flow with both feet. If you do want to jump ship now, you must slash your overhead to the bare minimum and probably even consider selling the house, moving into a low-cost apartment, have a paid-off car, so that you can stretch the amount of money you do have right now for as long as you can. Again, unless you are so unhappy in your job that you can't stand it anymore, and unless you do have some savings or the opportunity to move back with your parents and totally minimize your cost of living, I do not recommend you jump ship right away. Instead, I recommend you follow the part-time Wealth Wheel method. But who am I to recommend anything? It's your life and you've got to know what you want to do and how fast you want to go.

When my wife Michelle and I got started trying to take control of our financial lives, we had a great deal of debt. We had credit card debt, house debt, and two car payments. We owed payments on our couch, on our refrigerator, on our bed, our mattress—you name it. I did not make more per month than I spent. In other words, I was a model member of the American middle class living paycheck to paycheck.

The first step was becoming aware of where I was spending the money. I spent my money on travel. Travel was expensive, particularly to our respective home countries of Germany and Honduras. But it was part of our must-do list. We had committed not to lose contact with our families, so although I knew that it sucked all the savings from me, I committed to keep doing it. At the same time, that situation let me decide one of my reasons why—my motivator, my reason of why I needed to be financially independent. I wanted to be able to spend more time with my family.

Once I had reduced my variable expenses like cell phone bills, eating out, and the house electric bill, etc., to the limit, I realized that my way to financial security had to come almost entirely from earning more. I still was carrying quite a few loans I was making payments on. There were furniture loans, car loans, house mortgage, and student loans. Those were the next ones to tackle!

And that is what we did.

From every dollar of "extra money" we made, we used a small part to pay off these loans; another part we put into our separate seed money account. The majority of it, we put back into our growing land-flipping activities to buy more deals. When I finally was able to quit my job, we did something that you might consider strange but that illustrates our commitment to making it to financial independence fast.

By that time, we had paid off one car and all our consumer debt had gone. But we still had one car loan. Now that I was home all the time, we felt we didn't need the second car anymore. Instead of upgrading the first car, a seven year-old Geo Prizm, we sold the one-year-old nice car to get rid of the car payment. While the neighbors might have talked, we didn't care, and it didn't feel like a sacrifice to us. We still had a car. We still could get to and from wherever we wanted. My wife and I are inseparable, so we didn't need a second car. Wherever we went, we went together anyway. Why have a second payment that is not needed? For us, it made sense to eliminate that extra payment and reduce our monthly total expenses. It made us see the path to financial independence more clearly. It made it more achievable, and it made the step to quit my job easier and less scary. You know what? We kept driving that Geo Prizm for another four years. We probably would still be driving it if I had not totaled it in a small accident. It is easy to total a car that is only worth $2,500!

By the time the Geo was ready to go, we had built enough Temporary Cash and Forever Cash so that we could go from a Geo to a BMW X5 with all bells and whistles (and buy it with cash). Keeping expenses low while building up our income allowed us to go from our starter home to the home of our dreams.

We wanted to get to financial independence badly, so selling that second car was not a sacrifice. It was a liberating act on our end. By cutting our expenses to the bare minimum, we became the faster race car.

Learn the real lessons. Don't cut up your credit cards; that's not the solution.

- Cut back on what doesn't affect you.
- Switch to cheaper options of the same thing.
- Consider cutting back on a few larger things if you are hardcore.

- Focus, in parallel, on making more money and investing that money into Forever Cash Assets.

That combination will help get you where you want to be faster. It will allow you to take back the reigns to your life and decide the path of your life yourself, not have it decided by someone else.

That is truly what financial independence means to me.

It's the freedom of having choices.

It's the pride of having done what it takes to take care of your loved ones.

It's the freedom of being able to do what you want, when you want, and with whom you want without ever having to fear you will run out of money!

Chapter 16

FINDING CLARITY OF PURPOSE: THE WHY

What I have written here in this book I hope will rile you up a bit and make you evaluate the path you have taken so far. Perhaps, it might even make you want to change things in your life.

The next question is: How do you take action?

While I already talked about a few ways to get started, I think there is something important missing that I have not yet mentioned, and without that, any of your enthusiasm or anger will just evaporate without any action.

And that is what I call a Reason Why.

Everyone needs a Reason Why they should change what they are doing right now.

I hope I have shown you that if you follow the conventional wisdom given to you by the companies whose incentives are exactly opposite to yours, you are being screwed. You are being milked for your money. They are getting rich while you are stagnating. That should make you mad and give you some power to change things.

Without a reason, however, most people won't do anything.

Do you know anyone who is overweight and sick, knows it, and yet does nothing to change it?

Then, one day he has a heart attack, or one of their loved ones does, and overnight, he changes his ways and starts slimming down, starts running, and most importantly, keeps it up until he is in great shape. What made the difference? Why did it take a heart attack to change his behavior? The answer is *leverage*. Earlier I talked about good and bad debt and how leverage can be used in your favor or against you. A *why* is a different kind of non-monetary leverage you can use in your favor. The moment that person looked death in the eye, he realized that the price he was paying for his behavior was his own life. That was finally a powerful enough reason to change. He became scared to the core, and it created leverage to make him change his ways forever.

People do anything only for one of two reasons. They either want to get away from pain, or they want to get toward pleasure. When the person in the prior example realized that the bad habits of overeating or smoking were creating heart-attack-level pain, he was suddenly willing to do whatever it takes to get away from that pain. Before that, food was associated with pleasure, and, while there was some pain from being sick or obese, the pleasure of eating exceeded the pain of being sick. Now things are different. Eating poorly now is associated with pain and death, and eating healthily is associated with living. If that association was made strongly enough, the person will do anything to get away from that acute pain. If consequences are drastic enough, the new behavior will even stick long term.

But it doesn't have to be a heart attack that might make such a person change. It might be the birth of a child, and the realization (the pain) that he/she might never see that person grow up if he/she doesn't change those eating habits. Wanting to see the child grow up is something that has tremendous positive association, something that means tremendous pleasure. Therefore, if the promise of pleasure is big enough, it also can trigger a dramatic and lasting change in behavior.

But it only works if the person is aware of the reason why they need to change their behavior and see the consequences of their action or inaction—be it positive or negative.

So the *why* is the driving force behind lasting change and lasting success. This applies to every part of life, including your financial life. If you have a big enough reason *why* you need to be financially secure, independent, free and Forever Cash wealthy in exactly eighteen months or three years or five years from now, and if that reason is big enough, you will do what is needed to get there. The steps are easy, but many people don't do them because they don't have a Reason Why.

I can't overestimate the power of what I just wrote. Without a Reason Why, nothing will change!

"Get away from" reasons as motivation work when they are things you want to get away from like bad health, an abusive or stressful environment at work/home, fear of not having enough money to live on when you are old, etc. Such reasons are *very* powerful short term, but as soon as you have accomplished them, they tend to lose a lot of their power. As soon as you have created an environment where you have a better health or when you are able to change the job to something else (or quit it because of your cash flow income), there is a good chance you will stop staying on course.

"Going toward" values, goals, and reasons "why" are typically positive ones, like living in a certain house, or owning that special car or owning that boat that you have always wanted (but paid for with cash from your cash flow investments). Or, imagine having $100,000 a year or $200,000, or even $500,000 a year coming in in Forever Cash so that you can travel the world with your family. Picture yourself sipping a cocktail in your second home at the beach or being able to donate $100,000 a year to your favorite charity or your church. Those "going toward" reasons are your dreams of how life will be when you are financially secure.

Let me ask you something:

Why are you reading this far in this book? It's a simple question. Go ahead and take a moment to think about the answer.

Why do you want to create a Wealth Wheel and enjoy the freedom that comes with Forever Cash? Is it to retire early? To have more toys? To be able to leave something behind for your children and grandchildren after you die? Those are all good reasons to want to improve your financial lot in life. From my personal experience, in what I have lived and what I have seen, reasons like that may not be enough. They are too vague, and when the pressure is on, they won't stop you from falling back into bad habits.

You need to have a specific purpose.

Again, without a reason why you want to do this, chances are you won't do anything. Temptation will set in to spend the money, particularly once the amount of money you could access is more than you have ever had at your disposal, whatever that number might be. If you don't have a clear reason why you must reach this financial goal, life and your friends will pull you away, and you will give in to the temptation. The strongest way to prevent that is by having an overreaching reason *why* you must accomplish this that is *so* strong and *so* emotionally charged that it literally makes you freeze every time you are about to do something that sets you back.

Let me share with you an example from my own life. When I searched for the perfect way for me to make more money, I didn't give up, even though I was tired most nights. I literally spent hours each night searching, researching, and studying all kinds of ways to make more money until I found it. Sometimes I got back from work at midnight. Even then, I still sat for two more hours on the computer to figure things out.

Why? Because the thought of being stuck in this career traveling all the time, living in hotel rooms on hotel food, meeting with customers who didn't treat you well, and working with colleagues I had nothing in common with freaked me out. I so badly wanted to get away from that environment that I did whatever it took to accomplish it. That became my mantra and then Michelle's and my combined mantra. That mantra was "whatever it takes," "whatever it takes," "whatever it takes."

What will your mantra be?

You need a mantra to keep you motivated during the good times and the bad times. When you earn that first seed money, you need something to help you to fight the temptation to just go out and spend it. It needs to be something strong, something that matters in a guttural level, something that stops you in your tracks every time you want to go astray. Saying "I would like to retire sooner" will not be strong enough to keep you in line. It's not specific ("sooner" doesn't mean anything; it could be a day or a year or ten years), and it is not specific in quality (what does "retire" really mean? Retire with 100 percent of your current income? 200 percent? Or just 70 percent?) Be specific in your goal.

Create a reason why you just have to reach that goal. Be creative; paint a picture of you in your mind of being old and frail and not having enough money to eat. If you are security driven, that might do it. Fear is a powerful driver for short- and mid-term action. For me, it was the fear of being away from my family that did it.

On the positive side, draw a mental picture of your perfect life. Perhaps you are surrounded by your family, living in a castle, and all of you are successful, healthy people who are enjoying the best that life has to offer. All of this happened only because you changed the path of your life. You took some extra steps toward making extra money. You followed the Wealth Wheel concept. You made it happen. Perhaps that will do it. Make that picture, that scenario, that place in your life, *your* reason why you must do that. The more emotional you can make them, the better. Then, set a date for it.

Try to stack more reasons *why* on top of each other. If you have things that if you accomplish them would bring you to tears, ask yourself "why would that bring me to tears?" Dig deep, and try to find what motivates your desires. Once you discover that, you have found your real Reason Why. Imagine how you would like to truly live your life. If money weren't an issue, how would you spend your time each day? Would you become more involved in volunteer work or in working with your church? Would you dedicate your time to learning a profession and advancing mankind's knowledge in that field? Would you spend your days studying the love life of the South African ant? Is so, who cares if there's no money in it—you're not working for money anymore! If you could live such a life, what would it teach your kids; how would it set up your legacy? How would it make you feel? How badly do you want that feeling?

Flip to the other side. What would happen if it doesn't happen? What bad would happen? Ask yourself: Who would die without you being able to help them? Let that pain sink in and make the commitment to never, ever, *ever* let that happen as long as *you* have the power to change it.

I wish I had the money and the ability to get my grandparents to see the best doctors in the world when they were suffering from the cancer that ultimately killed them. But I didn't yet, and now that is one of my motivators to make sure I always have enough money to make sure my family will get the best medical care money can buy when and if they need it.

Remembering what you're trying to get away from and what you're going toward can be an effective tool for those moments during this process when you will be tempted to screw it all, take the money, and just buy something now with it.

In that moment, the purpose of Reason Why you are creating this comes into play. Go to my website at www.ForeverCash.com/why. Watch a video I have uploaded with a talk about when you know your Why, you are much more likely to have fun on the way and much more likely to get to it. Sacrifices you make turn into successful experiences because they help you get to where you want to go. Make sure you have a reason that's big enough to help you stick to your goals.

I am not you, and I don't know what motivates you.

Only *you* know that. Make a list of reasons why it is mandatory that you succeed during each phase of this process. Make some of them "getting away from" and some "going toward" reasons. Put those reasons somewhere that you are forced to see them every day. Each time you see them, they will be driven deeper and deeper into your consciousness, and you will be more and more committed.

Without the clarity of what the end goal is and why you want to get there, you probably won't reach your goal. You will probably give up long before. You are likely to get distracted on your way and end up in a different place, one where you never wanted to be, and many of your efforts will have been diluted.

Spend some time, alone or with your partner, to come up with a list of why you must change the situation you are in right now ("away" reasons) and why you must go toward a financially safe, independent place of abundance in life.

And once you found that reason *why* or a combination of *whys,* you won't have another choice but to move forward. It will become second nature.

CONCLUSION

You have made it to the last chapter of the book. You have had an opportunity to see how the truly wealthy think about money, how they strive for the third kind of cash, Forever Cash, and how financial advice from the world's leading financial industry should be taken critically and carefully to say the least. You have even seen how much of the conventional wisdom has been discarded long ago by the truly wealthy, who have their own way of making and using money by focusing on Forever Cash.

What should you do first?

As you will recall, the first thing you can address the fastest is to stop digging your way into a deeper financial hole. Start by playing financial defense. Find out how you can plug the drain of the bathtub, so that money stops escaping down the bottom. The point of this step will be to see if you can free up some money from your current full-time income. Start by taking a long, hard look at your spending habits.

- Make a list of all your expenses.
- Check to see if you can live without some of them.
- Schedule these expense reduction activities so that they actually happen. Put what you need to do to make these changes in your calendar. (Change your cell phone plan, cancel some subscriptions, etc.)
- Once you have played your defense and lowered your daily and monthly expenses, the next step will be to plan for the offense.
- Set up the two additional bank accounts, the Seed Money Account and the Fun Account.
- Create an automated mechanism to move the monthly savings from expense reductions into these accounts (an automatic bank transfer or withdrawal from your main account and deposit into the investment/Seed Money Account).
- Go through the chapter on how to earn extra money again. Do the exercise on how to find what you are good at, what you love doing, what you want to learn, and how to make money with that *outside* your job.
- Earn some extra seed money that, together with the money saved, will allow you to make some investments in cash-generating assets.

How can you start to make more income?

Ask yourself: What am I good at? What do I do already that other people would be willing to pay for? Am I a good writer? Can I provide services? What expertise do I have or can I develop that others are willing to pay for?

As for the next step, consider acquiring new skills that you can use to create extra cash on an ongoing basis for the next few years. What are people's problems, and what skill would you need to have to be able to solve them? What could I learn that people will need and will be willing to pay for? What profitable technique can you learn that can make you a bunch of money fast? What can you buy cheap and sell for more online? How does online marketing work? How does network marketing work?

How can you make money on the stock and options market without being exposed to massive risk?

If you are married, have a conversation with your spouse about how you can reshuffle priorities in your household so that one or both of you are freed up to make extra cash outside of work, or even at work by working extra hours if available. Think about small "businesses" that you could run from your home without much overhead and without employees. What do you enjoy doing that you would love to do more of? If you are handy, perhaps real estate fix and flip might be the right thing for you. Or perhaps being a handyman or a property manager might be an additional income source for you.

Once you have identified ways to make money short term, then *take action*. Get your first contractor gig and ask for referrals. Go apply for that second job. Ask your boss for more hours. Take on more responsibility at your job that ultimately will lead to a raise (note that money is an effect not the cause, just like you only get fire from a fireplace if you first put in a log and go through the effort of churning the fire. You want to do the new work first and then ask for a raise, not make the raise the condition for you doing the new work). If you would like to make more money part-time from home, take a class in Internet marketing or real estate investing. Ask around for information on what network marketing company is the best for you. (There are huge differences in reliability and concept.) Learn about stock market and options trading techniques.

While you do that, start working toward the third step of the process. Learn about investing in Forever Cash Assets that will provide you with passive income forever. While you are earning your seed money, make a list of Forever Cash Flow investment vehicles you want to learn more about. At my website, www.ForeverCash.com/education, you can join the free forum to discuss and get ideas and get plugged into our free community.

Start educating yourself about all things wealth and how it is being generated. Start educating yourself about how your wealth can be protected through tax-optimized structures, like corporations. I did not say much about the importance of using the proper legal structures to make money outside of your job and to invest in Temporary Cash and Forever Cash with, but having the right structures is immensely important. You can find out more about this subject at www.ForeverCash.com/entities.

Start educating yourself so that when opportunity presents itself you are ready to *act*, jump on it, and take the bull by its horns.

It's time to wake up and get active. Make sure you don't let this opportunity pass you by.

In summary, financial security, retirement, and your ability to quit your job are only possible in two ways:

- You build up such a large pile of cash that you won't be able to outspend it. Usually that takes a long time and, at the end, you are old, tired, and worn out. Plus, there is always the possibility of losing that money due to invariable market crashes or to bad decisions.
- You build up a stream of cash flow that will come in every month/quarter/year forever (i.e., Forever Cash) and which is high enough to cover your expenses while simultaneously getting rid of all your personal debt. The truly wealthy and the generationally wealthy have implemented Forever Cash and, as a result, they are completely debt free from all bad debt, yet they have large and ever-growing streams of Forever Cash Flow coming into their lives each month for the rest of their lives, their children's lives, and their children's children's lives.

That is the path my wife and I have taken, and it has been worth every inch of it. You can take the same path now that you understand that earn-to-spend is a dead-end street and truly a hamster wheel of financial hell. Forever Cash will not only enable you to quit your job, but it also will enable you to spend 24/7 with the ones you love. For me, that is my wife and daughter. I couldn't imagine being with anyone else more than them.

Forever Cash means peace of mind. It's the peace of mind from having to worry about whether you or your family will be able to eat next week, next month, or next year. Rest assured, you and they will. It's the peace of mind from having to worry about whether you or your family will have a place to live when you are old; you will. It's the peace of mind from whether you will be able to afford medication or medical care when you need it; you will. It's the peace of mind from having to worry about not being able to give your kids the best that life can give them—your time, attention, and love. You will. Forever Cash allows you to have the peace of mind to be able to be your best and give your best.

Forever Cash will allow you to travel the world to any place you like, whether that be romantic places like Paris or Venice or Rome, or more exotic places like Rio de Janeiro for Carnival—all in style without having to worry about money; or just take an RV and travel the United States for a year, like my friend and student did. Or, it allows you to just stay put, not work, relax at home, watch television all night and sleep all day, or just do whatever you want to do in life— including doing absolutely nothing—if that is what you desire.

But this is not just about us or you. Forever Cash has enabled us to not just be financially independent but also to help others around us. It has helped us to support the causes we believe in. For example, a number of schools for the poor in Honduras have been helped with our donations. One donation, a substantial amount, was used to build an entire kindergarten building where now little four- and five-year-old kids who otherwise would have no chance in life are being taught the first skills of their life, and are bilingual in English and Spanish. Forever Cash has helped us to help family members who needed our assistance. It has paid for airline tickets for us to fly across the country or across the ocean when loved ones needed us. Thanks to Forever Cash, we were able to be there by their side when they needed us. We didn't have to say, "Sorry, we can't afford to come." We didn't think twice and just booked a flight, hotel, and rental car—and even paid for hospital stays. It didn't make a dent in our bank account. That is your future if you engage in this process.

It is simple to do, all you need is to start seeing the world from the eyes of the truly rich, the generationally rich who use Forever Cash principles, and then follow the described steps. Most importantly, when you absorb, internalize and apply these concepts, you will grow your wealth with ease. It will become second nature.

Forever Cash is the solution that will bring you to financial independence.

ABOUT THE AUTHOR

Jack Bosch is an entrepreneur, nationally recognized speaker, and wealth mentor who became a cash and Forever Cash millionaire through real estate investments and online businesses. A German immigrant, Jack left his job after a corporate downturn in search for security and the American dream of wealth. Within eighteen months, he reached his goal by discovering the Forever Cash wealth philosophy.

An active real estate investor since 2003 and respected investment trainer since 2008, Jack has reached tens of thousands of entrepreneurs around the world with his best-selling training programs including: "The Land Profit Generator," "The Hidden Tax Sale Cash System," and "Online Selling Fortunes." Through his training sessions and seminars, Jack educates his students on the secrets to creating and maintaining true lasting generational wealth.

Through the diligent application of the Forever Cash philosophy, Jack was, by the age of thirty-four, in the position to retire. Instead, he set upon a mission to help other individuals achieve their financial goals. Jack believes anyone, no matter the age or the situation, can become and stay wealthy within three to five years in their own business—even if they are working full time starting with little money or assets. Jack shares his proven wealth strategies for creating a life of abundance in Forever Cash. For more information, visit his websites at ForeverCash. com and JackBosch.com.

ENDNOTES

1   Mark Cuban, "Success and Motivation—You Only Have to Be Right Once!" Blogmaverick.com, May 30, 2005, accessed December 10, 2012, http://blogmaverick.com/2005/05/30/success-and-motivation-you-only-have-to-be-right-once/.

2   Pablo S. Torre, "How (and Why) Athletes Go Broke," *SI Vault,* March 29, 2009, http://sportsillustrated.cnn.com/vault/article/magazine/MAG1153364, accessed May 21, 2013.

3   Warren Buffett as quoted by Dang Le, Emory University MBA student, from Q&A session with Warren Buffett, "Notes from Buffett Meeting 2/15/2008," *Underground Value,* February 23, 2008, accessed May 21, 2013, http://undergroundvalue.blogspot.com/2008/02/notes-from-buffett-meeting-2152008_23.html.

4   "As Job Market Mends, Dropouts Fall Behind," The Wall Street Journal online, February 21, 2012, accessed May 21, 2013, http://online.wsj.com/article/SB100014240529702033158045772111190378957930.html.

5   Morgan Korn, "America's Retirement System Is Failing Us: Economist," finance.yahoo.com, August 6, 2012, accessed December 31, 2012, http://finance.yahoo.com/blogs/daily-ticker/america-retirement-system-failing-us-economist-153445894.html.

6   Joel Schlesinger, "Reality TV Villain Writes about Life and Money in New Autobiography," *The Winnipeg Free Press.* October 1, 2011, accessed December 20, 2012, http:// www.winnipegfreepress. com/opinion/columnists/the-dragons-pen-130900253.html.

Exclusive Bonus For Readers Only...

Get Your Free 'Forever Cash' Planning Kit!

Yours Free:
A $197
Value!

As a special thank you gift for reading this book, I invite you to claim your FREE Forever Cash Planning Kit! This set of resources gives you valuable tools and guidance to help you start building Forever Cash flowing into your life.

When you register to claim your free gift, at the website below, you'll receive:

- **The "Forever Cash Life Assessment":** A self-assessment that helps you determine how you are doing right now and which Forever Cash sources best fit your goals and life going forward. After completing your Forever Cash Life Assessment, you'll be sent a special report based on your answers.
- **The "Wealth Wheel Blueprint":** This detailed printable blueprint of my Wealth Wheel process will give you a clear overview of the step by step program to obtain Financial Independence through Forever Cash.
- **Two Forever Cash Analysis Worksheet:** Use this to pinpoint your income vs. out-go, and guide your spending to meet your Forever Cash goals.
- **Forever Cash Investment Analysis:** This tool allows you to make informed decisions about your investments and assets. Just enter the necessary information about your existing or planned investments and it automatically tells you if it's a winner based on ROI and Cash on Cash Return! (No math needed!)
- **Access to the Forever Cash Community:** You'll have access to our online group of success driven Forever Cash Community Members, so you can discuss the topics of this book, as well as network with other like-minded people from all around the world.

All together this amazing package will be crucial to your success in generating Forever Cash. And as a reader, please accept this kit as a gift for your time and commitment.

To claim the Forever Cash Planning Toolkit including all of the free gifts listed above, simply register at the web address below. Claim your instant access now:

www.ForeverCash.com/Gift

CPSIA information can be obtained at www.ICGtesting.com
Printed in the USA
BVOW08s0829080813

327722BV00002B/7/P